# NETCOMICS Manhwa Sampler

Spring 2007

# NETCOMICS Manhwa Sampler
# Spring 2007

---

English translation rights in USA, Canada, UK, NZ, Australia arranged by
Ecomix Media Company
395-21 Seogyo-dong, Mapo-gu, Seoul, Korea 121-840 info@ecomixmedia.com

- Produced by Ecomix Media Company
- Editors Jeffrey Tompkins, Jim Scaife, Nick Anders, Philip Daay
- Managing Editor Soyoung Jung
- Cover Design purj
- Graphic Design Hyekyoung Choi, Eunsook Lee
- President & Publisher Heewoon Chung

P.O. Box 16484, Jersey City, NJ 07306
info@netcomics.com
www.NETCOMICS.com



**ISBN: 978-1-60009-195-7**

Printed in Korea
January 2007

## Discover the best in manhwa at NETCOMICS.com!

NETCOMICS is proud to present the finest selection of online & book-form manhwa titles from Korea.

From fist-clenching drama to heart-aching romance, provocative science fiction to one-of-a-kind comedy, mind-boggling thrillers to ground-breaking new format web comics, NETCOMICS offers a complete manhwa collection of every genre for all ages.

All of these titles and more are available for online reading, and their first chapters are absolutely free. Visit netcomics.com today and taste our rich selection of extraordinary manhwa titles!

## Contents



Release dates, prices and specifications are subject to change.

NETCOMICS P.O. Box16484, Jersey City, NJ 07306 www.netcomics.com support@netcomics.com

# ALMOST HIGHLY CLASSIFIED

by JTK

A chaotic uproar of the Almost Highly Classified Team members who settle in a remote beachside village! Tom Anjery, vice-chief of the Almost Highly Classified Team at the GIS (Global Intelligence Services), receives an order to relocate the team's office and privately operate it independent of the GIS, due to a budget reduction. The team gets a new office in a remote village, but to appropriate the operational funds on their own, they decide to hold two jobs. With his confidants, Jay Biel, Warren X, and Louis Legstrong, Tom arranges a bar on the first floor and an office on the 2nd floor of their new building and barely manages them. Meanwhile, the Baywatch team that patrols the beach casts a doubtful eye at them, and the team leader Sergio Ciprani especially gets on bad terms with Tom and his team. *Almost Highly Classified* is a hilarious fusion of CSI and Dumb & Dumber.

- **Comedy for Age 13+**

"IT'S FRESH TO SEE COMICS ON AN ALMOST FBI-LIKE SUBJECT. VERY FUNNY."

*– Lola Hachinana, NETCOMICS subscriber*

WITH THE TEAM'S INJURIES AS AN EXCUSE
EPISODE #22.
A WOMAN WHO READS MINDS

THE INVESTIGATION ON THE WOMAN WHO CAN SEE THOUGHTS

WAS DUMPED ONTO THE ROOKIE AGENT.

RIGHT HERE.

SCREECH

I'VE COME FROM THE GIS.
SIR, YOU'RE THE ONE WHO PHONED IN, RIGHT?

YES... BUT HASN'T DEPUTY DIRECTOR TOM ANJERY COME WITH YOU?
YOU KNOW THE DEPUTY DIRECTOR?

HE'S BEEN THE LIGHT OF MY LIFE... I'M A FOLLOWER OF HIS.

HAVE YOU READ THIS BOOK? "MYSTERIES! WHY THE HECK IN THE WORLD," TOM ANJERY, DEPUTY DIRECTOR, WROTE IT.
UNLIKE OTHER MYSTERY BOOKS, WITH NO BASIS IN FACT...

THE BOOK THAT DEPUTY DIRECTOR ANJERY HAS WRITTEN TAKES AN EVIDENCE-CENTERED, RATIONAL APPROACH.
Mysteries!
he heck in the world.
TOM ANJERY

I WANTED TO MEET HIM TODAY AND LISTEN TO HIS VIEWS... THAT'S TOO BAD.

UMM... THE REPORT YOU'VE PUT IN...
OH, RIGHT!

I SHOULD INTRODUCE MYSELF FIRST.
MY NAME IS BROKE BACKMOUNTAIN. I RUN THE FARM THAT WE'VE HAD SINCE MY FATHER'S TIME.

THIS IS SUCH A REMOTE PLACE THAT THE ONLY PERSON WHO VISITS IS A COWBOY FRIEND OF MINE NAMED GERE ASFORK...
I LIVE HERE WITH MY YOUNGER SISTER, BRANGELINA.
YOU SAID SHE'S THE PERSON WHO COULD SEE OTHER PEOPLE'S THOUGHTS, RIGHT?

MY SISTER HAS LIKED TO DRAW EVER SINCE SHE WAS YOUNG.
SHE WANTED TO BECOME A PAINTER.

IT'S PROBABLY BEEN ABOUT A MONTH SINCE THE STRANGE ABILITY THAT I PHONED IN ABOUT STARTED.

ALL THE PAINTINGS HANGING ON THE WALL ARE BRANGELINA'S WORK.

BRANGELINA, THE PERSON FROM THE GIS I TOLD YOU ABOUT IS HERE.
SHE SAYS SHE'S COME TO CONFIRM WHETHER YOU REALLY HAVE THE ABILITY TO SEE OTHER PEOPLE'S THOUGHTS.

WHY DON'T YOU GO IN AND HAVE A TALK WITH HER.

HELLO.

YES...
COME IN.

BRANGELINA BACKMOUNTAIN EXPLAINED THE PHENOMENON THAT HAD HAPPENED TO HER.

YOU'VE PROBABLY HEARD FROM MY BROTHER, BUT THIS IS A LONESOME PLACE.

THERE ARE LOTS OF TIMES WHEN NO ONE STOPS BY FOR DAYS.
THE ONLY REASON I COULD PUT UP WITH A PLACE LIKE THIS IS...

BECAUSE THERE WAS GERE.
GERE, YOUR BROTHER'S FRIEND?

GERE WAS HANDSOME...
AND KIND.

MY BROTHER, GERE, AND I...THE THREE OF US HAD GOOD TIMES TOGETHER.

I STARTED TO HAVE SPECIAL FEELINGS FOR GERE.
I IMAGINED A HAPPY FUTURE TOGETHER WITH HIM.

IT'S NOT A PUSH-UP BRA!
THESE BREASTS ARE REAL!
I'M SORRY?

THAT'S WHAT YOU WERE THINKING JUST NOW, WHEN YOU LOOKED AT ME!

ANYWAY... ONE EVENING IN THE KITCHEN I WAS LOOKING BLANKLY AT MY BROTHER, WHO WAS BAKING AN APPLE PIE...

I COULD SEE WHAT MY BROTHER WAS THINKING, LIKE I WAS WATCHING A MOVIE.

BRANGELINA IS TELLING YOU THE TRUTH.
WHAT'S THE SUPERLAME COUPLE THAT I DON'T EVER WANNA SEE AGAIN BUTTING IN HERE FOR?!

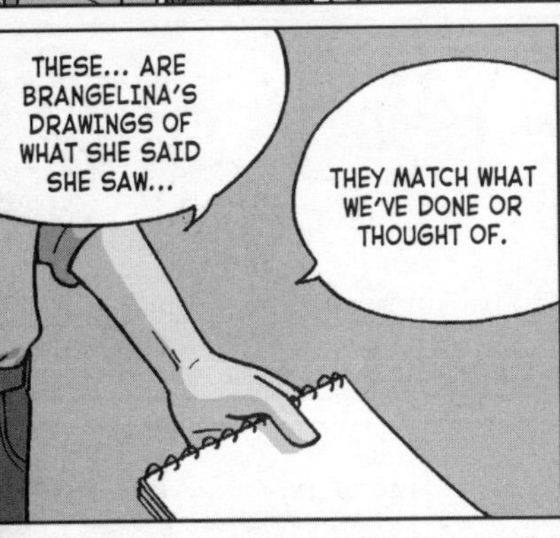
THESE... ARE BRANGELINA'S DRAWINGS OF WHAT SHE SAID SHE SAW...
THEY MATCH WHAT WE'VE DONE OR THOUGHT OF.

HMM...
WELL... IT'S HARD TO PROVE SHE HAS THE ABILITY TO SEE THOUGHTS WITH JUST THESE DRAWINGS...

ALRIGHT THEN! I'M GOING TO SEE YOUR THOUGHTS NOW.
THINK OF THE HOUSE THAT YOU LIVE IN.

HOUSE?

SHE'LL DRAW IT PERFECTLY.
HOUSE...
......

I C...CAN'T DRAW IT, WHY WON'T YOU THINK OF YOUR HOME?

UMM... ACTUALLY I HAVE AMNESIA... I DON'T EVEN KNOW WHERE MY HOME IS.
WHAT?

OH... AND... I'VE ONLY BECOME A GIS AGENT TODAY...
SO IT'S HARD FOR ME TO MAKE A DETERMINATION MYSELF.

FOR NOW, I'LL CALL HEADQUARTERS FIRST.
HEY. IS THIS SOME KIND OF BAD JOKE?

GIS

CHIEF, THE ROOKIE JUST CALLED.
MM, IS THAT SO?

THE WOMAN SHE MET TODAY...

IS SHE HOT?
AL INTELIGENCE SERVIC

SAYS SHE'S A LOOKER.

TA TA TA
TOM ANJERY, DEPUTY DIRECTOR, MAKES AN EMERGENCY BUDGET ADJUSTMENT!!
ALMOST HIGHLY CLASSIFIED TEAM ARRIVES ON-SITE WITHIN 30 MINUTES!!
GENTLEMEN! THIS IS AN IMPORTANT CASE, SO PROCEED WITH CAUTION--NO RASH BEHAVIOR!

## *Madtown Hospital*

by JTK

Korea's #1 comedy author and his genre-defining masterpiece *Madtown Hospital* are invading the U.S.! Prepare to overdose on laughter as you enter JTK's aptly named Hospital and meet its staff of quirky characters.

- **Comedy/Humor for Age 13+**

## *Hotel California*

by JTK

Free of charge and all-inclusive, Collin Prison, otherwise known as "Hotel California," will take any troublemaker whatsoever who arrives...and will try to reform him to boot! Sit back and watch a bizarre cast of characters as they work up a non-stop series of absurd and hilarious events guaranteed to have you rolling on the floor.

- **Comedy/Humor for All Ages**

## *X Diary*

by Toma

Mingo is a 26-year-old cartoonist with a fiery temper who breaks up with her easygoing musician boyfriend Jerry. They decide to stay friends, even though they still have feelings for each other. A sagacious and sarcastic journey that will get your head nodding and face smiling.

- **Comedy/Humor for All Ages**

by Youjung Lee

Perverto is just a regular 17-year-old... with the unavoidable nickname, "pervert." To escape his bad reputation, he transfers to a new school for a fresh start. But on his first day there, he's falsely accused of groping a girl named Hongdan on the subway. To make matters worse, she happens to be another new student who has just transferred to his new school, to his very class. The real pervert who framed him is a math teacher at his new school, too! The teacher is an expert at getting away with perverted behavior... and he's targeted Hongdan for more gropes. The girl possesses a voluptuous body and mysterious bruises, and Perverto is smitten with her. Will he survive his new school? The true nature of perverto wiggles to the surface in volume 1 of this sexy new series!

- **Comedy for Age 16+**

"...HUMOROUS, PROVIDES AN INTERESTING CONCEPT..."

*– Katrina Christopher, NETCOMICS subscriber*

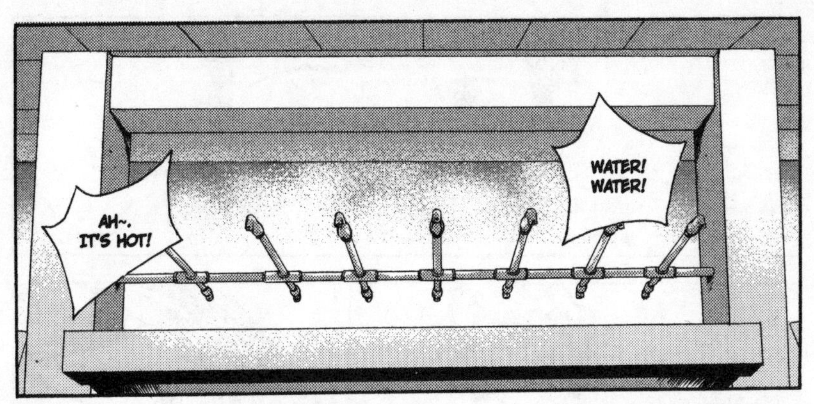
WATER! WATER!
AH~. IT'S HOT!

STAND IN LINE!!
STAND IN LINE! KEEP IN LINE!
P.E. DURING SUMMER IS HELL!

WHOO-

AH... REFRESHING~.
HUFF HUFF
... HOT~.

!
H...HEY. YOU GOTTA THINK OF THE PERSON BEHIND YOU.

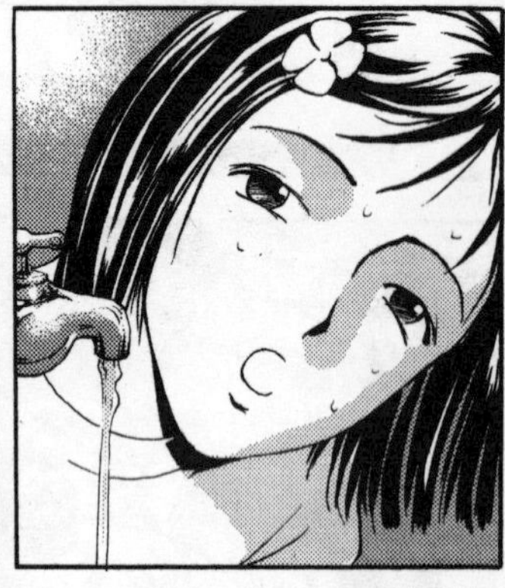

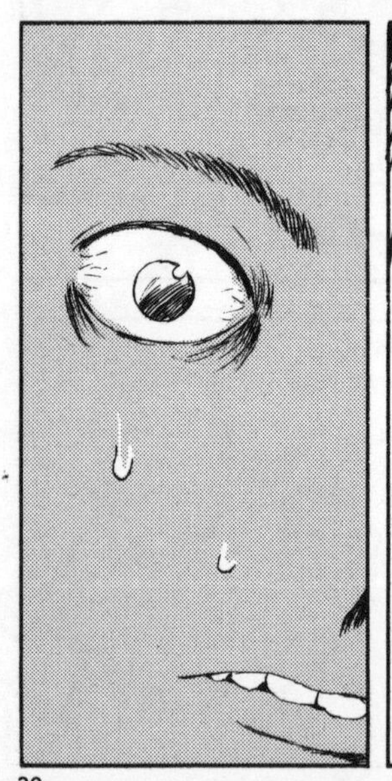

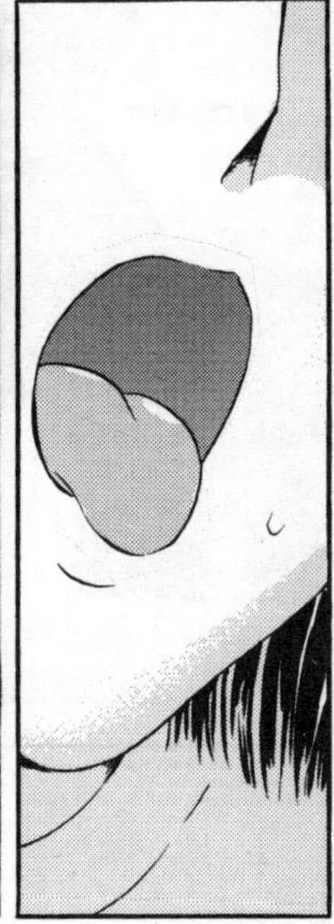

OH...
NO....
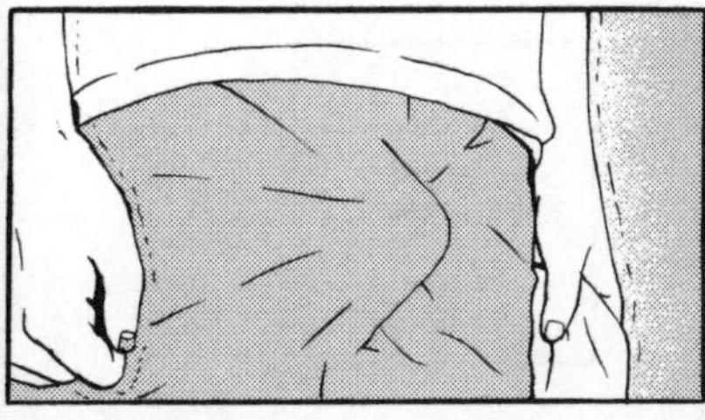

HEY... CHECK THAT OUT.
HUH? WHAT'S UP WITH THIS JOKER?

YOU PERVERT!
WHAT ARE WE GONNA DO WITH YOU?!
WHAT'S ON YOUR DIRTY MIND?
EEK~. PERVERT!
PERVERT!
ONCE AGAIN, THAT SUMMER...
THE WORD "PERVERT" STUCK WITH ME WITHOUT FAIL.

# CHAPTER 1

I. CAN. DO. IT!!

I LOVE YOU, JINYOUNG
I CAN DO THIS!

I'M GOING TO FORGET THE PAST...

AND START A NEW LIFE HERE.
BING

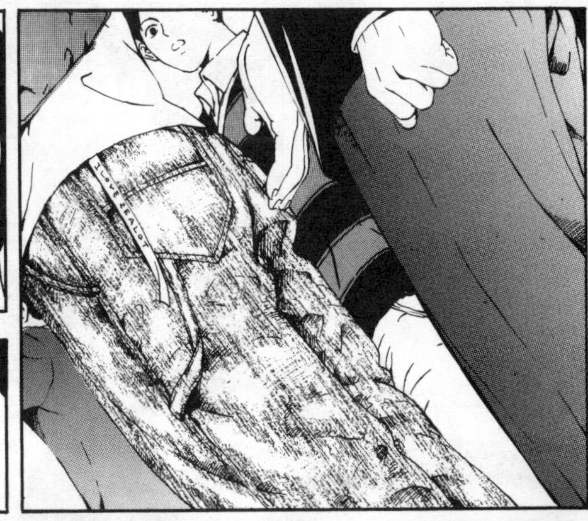

YES, START OVER...
HEE HEE...

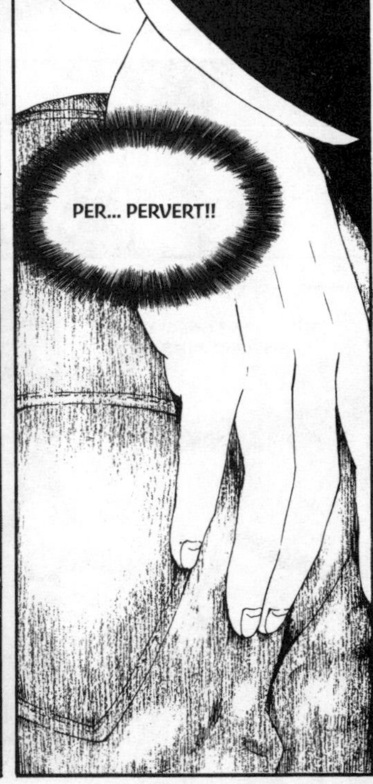
PER... PERVERT!!

THUMP
THUMP
GASP...!!
TH...THAT...!!

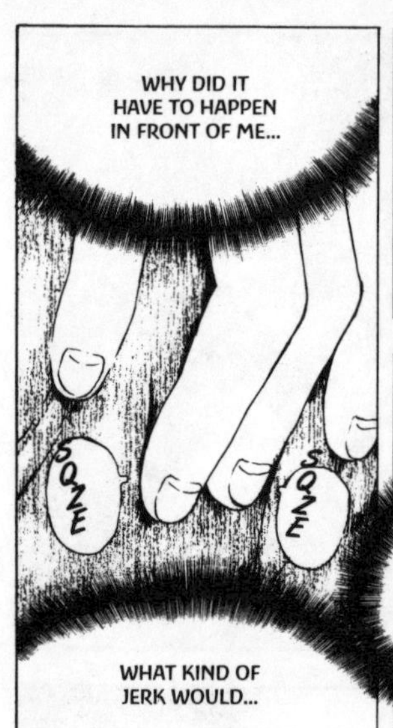
WHY DID IT HAVE TO HAPPEN IN FRONT OF ME...
SQZE
SQZE
WHAT KIND OF JERK WOULD...

......

A POKER FACE AND A GOATEE...
RUB RUB
HOW COULD HE...

THAT'S NO ORDINARY HAND MOVEMENT TECHNIQUE. HE'S NO BUNGLER, HE'S A PRO.
THUMP
THUMP
WHAT DO I DO? DAMN IT...

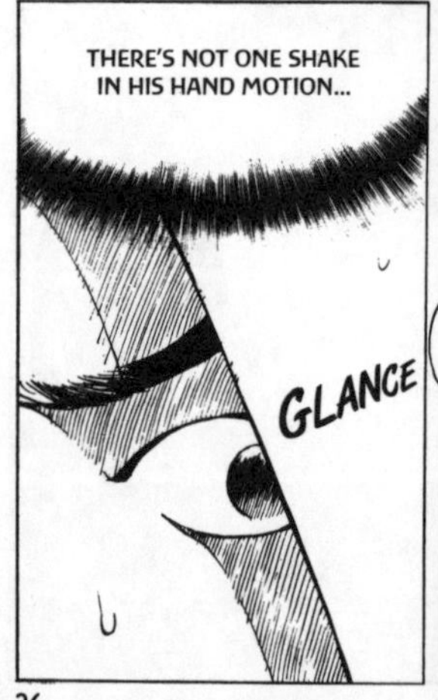
THERE'S NOT ONE SHAKE IN HIS HAND MOTION...
GLANCE

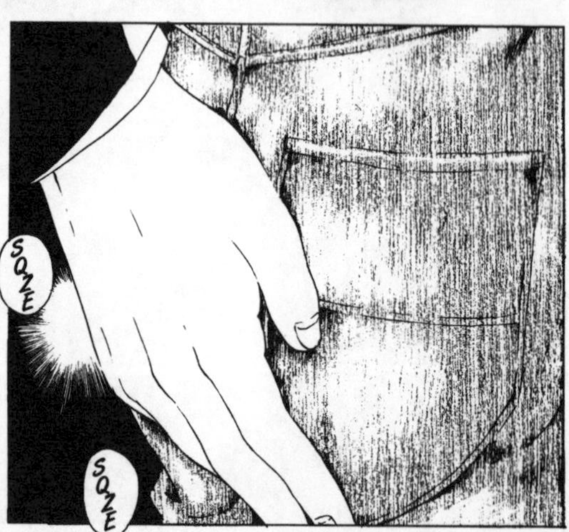
SQZE
SQZE

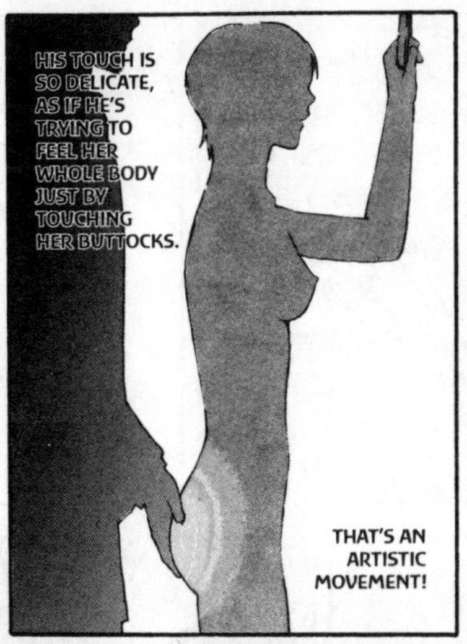

HIS TOUCH IS SO DELICATE, AS IF HE'S TRYING TO FEEL HER WHOLE BODY JUST BY TOUCHING HER BUTTOCKS.
THAT'S AN ARTISTIC MOVEMENT!

WHAT AM I THINKING?!! ...THE GUY'S A PERVERT!
HE'S HUMAN TRASH! I CAN'T LET MYSELF GET PULLED IN!

YES! THIS TIME, I'LL SHOW EVERYONE THAT I'M NOT A PERVERT!
IF I GET THAT PERVERT ARRESTED BY THE POLICE, THEN I'LL BE THE GOOD YOUNG MAN!!

HEH HEH! THAT'S IT! I'LL CATCH HIM IN THE ACT!
GULP
RIGHT NOW!

HEY~, MISTER!!

...?

CAN'T YOU HEAR ME?! MISTER PERVERT!!

YOU SHOULD MOVE THAT HAND!!

SQUEESH

GOTCHA!!

SQUEESH?
? ? ? ? ? ? ?

......

......
WHAT'S THI
COUNTRY
COMIN' TO
LITTLE PUNK!
GRRR
YOU PERVERT.
Y...YOU DON'T UNDERSTAND.
I... I'M

I...I'M..

YOU DIDN'T...

...HAVE TO GO THAT FAR.

I WAS GONNA LET IT GO...
IT... IT'S NOT LIKE THAT.

PHOOK
PHOOK
BUT I CAN'T FORGIVE...
A JERK LIKE YOU ANYMORE!!
POW POW
THUD
OOF.
WHA...WHAT THE HELL IS HAPPENING?!
PHTOOP
THIS STATION IS...
THE DOORS...

I WAS GONNA BE PATIENT TODAY NO MATTER WHAT...

BUT THERE'S A LIMIT TO MY PATIENCE!

......

DON'T MESS WITH ME AGAIN!

THIS IS DRIVING ME CRAZY...

BEING MISTAKEN FOR A PERVERT ON MY FIRST DAY...

.......

ARGH... THIS DOESN'T LOOK GOOD.

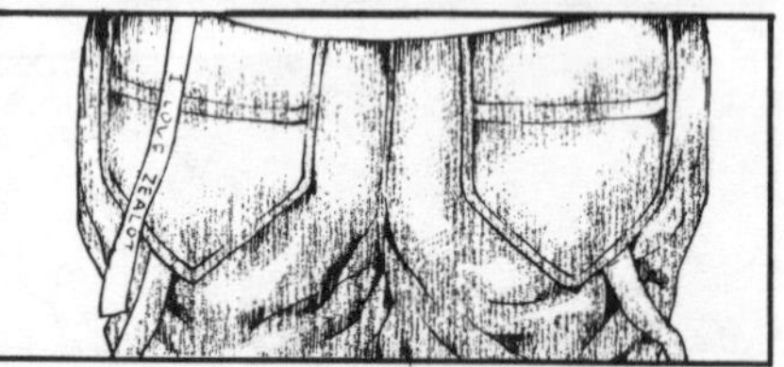

GASP

I...I WAS JUST...

STOP FOLLOWING ME, YOU PERVERT!

......

IF YOU CROSS THIS STREET, YOU'RE DEAD!!

IS SHE RUNNING AWAY THIS TIME...?
BUT I HAVE TO GO THIS WAY, TOO.
AND ANYWAY, THAT'S THE TYPE OF FIGURE...
THAT PERVERTS WOULD REALLY DIG.
SHIT, WHAT AM I THINKING?!
SHOCK
I AM DEFINITELY NOT A PERVERT!!
I'M LATE! AND I HAVE TO RUN AT LEAST 100 METERS TO CROSS THE OVERPASS!
HUFF!
HUFF!
MY MORNING'S RUINED BECAUSE OF THAT BUTCH!
HAA.
HAA.
I'M LATE! I'M LATE!!

...IS THIS IT?

HA-AH.

HA-AH.

HA-AH.

OH, YEAH~!

THE PLACE WHERE I'LL LIVE OUT THE REST OF MY HIGH SCHOOL DAYS!!

I SHOULDN'T BE THINKING ABOUT THAT NOW!
WHERE'S CLASSROOM 8...
NOW, BEFORE WE BEGIN
OUR CLASS TODAY, I WOULD ESPECIALLY
LIKE TO INTRODUCE...
CREAK
GOOD MORNING, TEACHER!!
I'M SORRY I'M LATE!
AH~. YOU'RE JUST IN TIME.
WE WERE WAITING FOR YOU.
YES~. SORRY FOR BEING LATE.
IT'S OKAY. YOU'RE NOT THAT LATE~.

THEN...
WHO WANTS TO GO FIRST AND INTRODUCE THEMSELVES?

WOW~. SHE'S BEAUTIFUL!♡

HRN? WHAT DOES SHE MEAN?

STUMP

MY NAME IS HONGDAN.

GLAD TO MEET YOU.

# 10, 20, and 30

*by Morim Kang*

*Cover not final

Three extraordinary women in three age groups and three unforgettable lives intersect in Morim Kang's fascinating *10, 20, and 30*. Yuhrin is a clumsy, scatterbrained widow in her 30's whose teenage daughter, Kangae, is forced to take care of. Meanwhile, Kangae's jaded, twenty-something cousin, Ami suffers a messy breakup with her boyfriend. Finally, Kangae, who dreads the thought of growing up and its attendant responsibilities, hates men and is sure to complicate matters. Get ready for one wild ride with *10, 20, and 30*.

- **Drama/Romance for Age 16+**

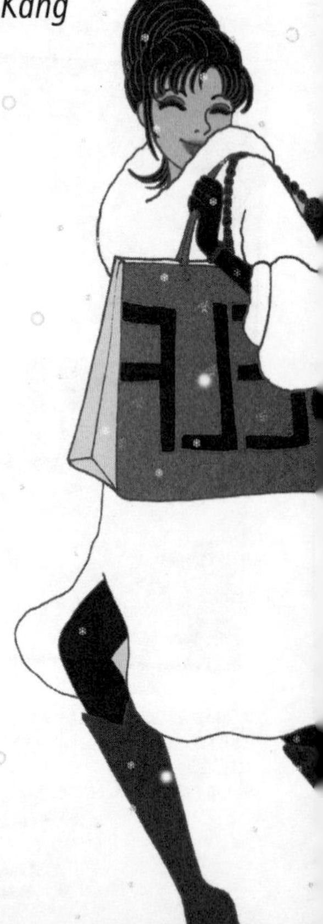

SHOWER CREAM
BATH
THIRD STORY
NO19
THWAP
FLAP
FLAP

WASHED OUT DESIGNS WITH DULL COLORS...

TRY IT AGAIN! ALTHOUGH I DON'T THINK YOU'LL DO ANY BETTER.

UM...

?

I DON'T KNOW WHY I'M SINGLED OUT AS YOUR PUNCHING BAG! WHY ARE YOU DOING THIS TO ME?

WHA... WHAT?
I WAS REFLECTING THE NOW POPULAR RETRO MOVEMENT IN THOSE DESIGNS. I WAS PROUD OF THEM.

YOU UGLY WITCH, HYSTERICAL OLD MAID!
WHY YOU FOUR-EYED WIDOW! ARE YOU CRAZY?

WHAT? YES.
WHAT ARE YOU STARING AT? LEAVE AND GET BACK TO WORK.
?

HURRY
SCURRY

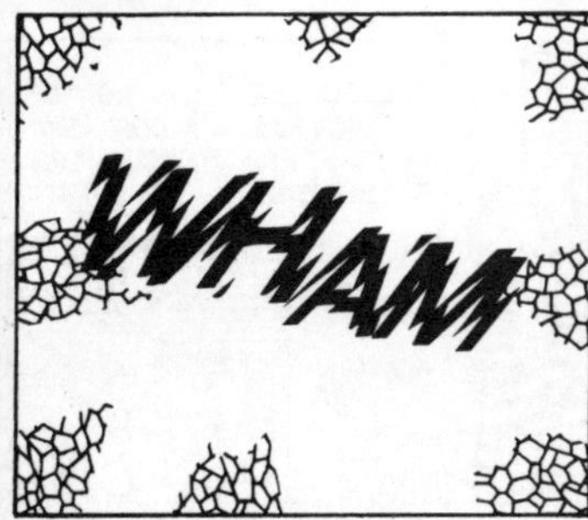
WHAM

MR. CHOI!
OH NO, ARE YOU ALRIGHT?

......
......

I'M SORRY! I'M SORRY!

......

HEY- MS. NOH! HOW ARE YOU?
OH, MR. CHOI!

LATELY <MIME> HAS BECOME THE MOST POPULAR BRAND IN OUR COMPANY. I HAVE YOU TO THANK, MS. NOH!
WHY, THANK YOU...

IT'S BECAUSE YOU CARE ABOUT OUR TEAM VERY MUCH...
SO I HAVE YOU TO THANK TOO, MR. CHOI- HUHUHU

SHE'S SUCH A FLIRT, IT'S DISGUSTING!
IT LOOKS LIKE MS. NOH HAS FEELINGS FOR THE BIG BOSS!
NO! NO! DON'T SAY SICK STUFF LIKE THAT!

?

YUHRIN, WHAT ARE YOU DOING?
OH, JUST COFFEE...

SLAM
SO THE PUBLIC RELATIONS TEAM WANTED DISCUSS THE ADVERTISEMENT ISSUE...
I HAD SEVERAL IDEAS I WANTED TO SUGGEST, THIS IS GOOD.

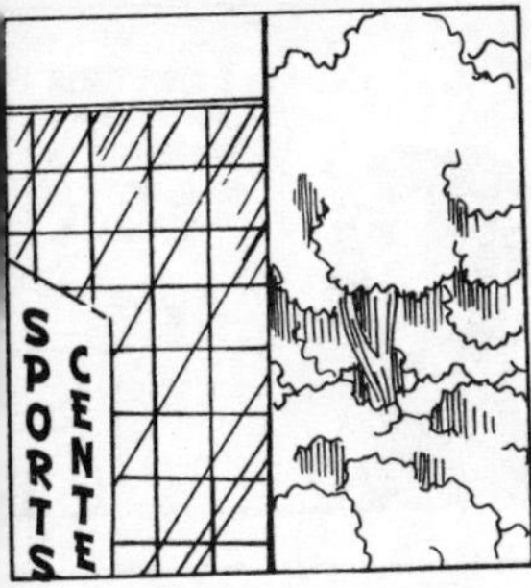
SPORTS CENTE

NOT HERE...?

HERE
THERE

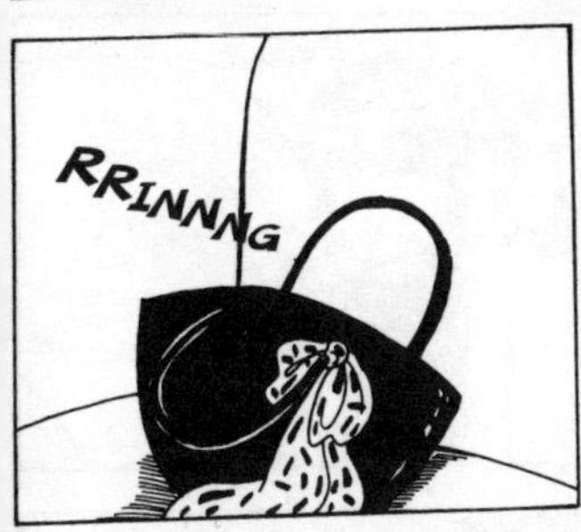
RRINNNG

YES-?

MOM!
WHERE THE HELL ARE YOU? YOU SURE YOU'RE NOT WITH A MAN RIGHT NOW?

MOM! MY BODY IS AS PURE AS VIRGIN SNOW, SO DON'T YOU WORRY.

SHUT UP! YOUR FATHER IS ABOUT TO LOSE HIS TEMPER RIGHT NOW!
WHY?

BECAUSE YOU RAN AWAY FROM THE BLIND DATE I ARRANGED FOR YOU!
I DIDN'T RUN AWAY! I WAS THERE FOR AN HOUR, WAITING FOR HIM.
24
BY

DON'T YOU LIE TO ME! THE GUY SAID HE WAITED FOR YOU FOR AN HOUR, TOO!
I TOLD YOU, I DON'T KNOW WHAT HAPPENED.

I GUESS I HAVE NO CHOICE BUT TO GO TO SEOUL TOMORROW!
WAIT, MOM! NO!

JEEZ, I'M SICK OF THIS. IS THERE NO SUCH THING AS COMPLETE FREEDOM?
24
BY

CHOMP
CHOMP
BOOP

RING~

WHO PAGED ME?
IT'S ME, AMI! WHERE YOU AT?

SOME TV STUDIO! I CAME TO INTERVIEW THIS MANAGER DUDE,
BUT HE'S NOT HERE! THEY SAID HE'S ON A BUSINESS TRIP. DAMN!
GUESS YOU'RE IN THE SAME BOAT AS ME.

THEN SHOULD WE MEET UP?
FINE! I'LL SEE YOU AT THE USUAL PLACE.

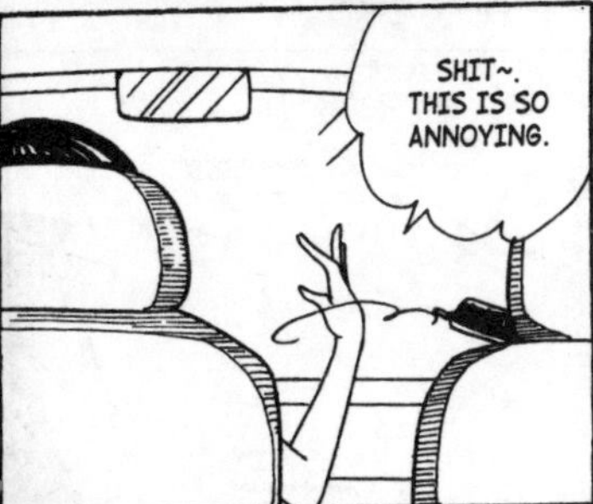
SHIT~. THIS IS SO ANNOYING.

WHY THE HELL DID I PAGE BEAU WHEN I DON'T EVEN WANT TO SEE HIM?
I'M INSANE!

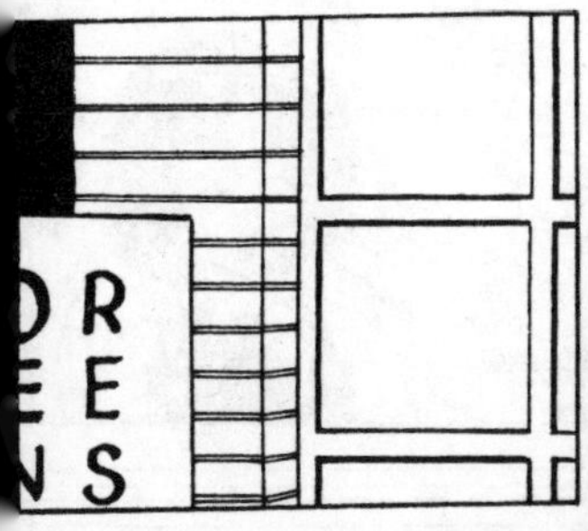
R
RES
NS

WHAT WILL YOU HAVE? I'LL PAY!
FORGET IT. I'LL PAY FOR MY OWN FOOD.

BUT I WANT TO TREAT YOU TO DINNER.
YOU'RE NO MILLIONAIRE, SO THERE'S NO NEED FOR YOU TO GO OVERBOARD!!

...... ♪
I'LL HAVE THE FILET MIGNON WITH ONION SOUP...
ITALIAN DRESSING...

WHAT WILL YOU HAVE? WHY DON'T YOU MARK IT DOWN TO YOUR LEVEL AND GET CHICKEN BREASTS? YOU LIKE BOOBS, DON'T YOU?

UNFORTUNATELY, IT SEEMS LIKE THEY DON'T HAVE YOUR ALL TIME FAVORITE, THE BUTTOCKS.
FLUSHED

WHAT'S THE MATTER WITH YOU?
WHAT DID I DO?

ARE YOU TRYING TO PICK A FIGHT WITH ME OR SOMETHING?
PICK A FIGHT? ABOUT WHAT?

AREN'T YOU TRYING TO SAY THAT YOU'RE TIRED OF ME, SO YOU WANT TO BREAK UP?
UGLY KIDS SURE ARE GOOD AT GUESSING!

HEY!!

HIC... HIC...
HIC... HIC...
......

DRINK WATER!
GULP
GULP

LET'S GET MARRIED.
!

HIC HIC
HIC HIC
HIC HIC

I'VE SLEPT WITH YOU MORE THAN ONE HUNDRED TIMES! THEREFORE, YOU'RE MINE.
I WAS A VIRGIN, AND YOU WERE MY FIRST WOMAN! SO I'M AFRAID YOU'LL HAVE TO TAKE RESPONSIBILITY.

HIC... HIC...
HIC... HIC...
HIC... HIC...
SILENCE!
SLAM

EEP

WHERE'S THE GREEN ONIONS?

TISK, TISK! YOU SHOULD HAVE TRIMMED THE GREEN ONIONS AND PUT IT IN THE FRIDGE.

ANYWAY, WHAT'S THE NAME OF THIS DISH?
STEW HOTPOT.

NEVER HEARD OF IT BEFORE.
......

LAST NIGHT I SAW SOMEONE WHO WAS A LOT LIKE YOU!
A LOT LIKE ME?

YEAH! HE WAS SLOPPY, CLUMSY, AND CONFUSED.

DO I LOOK THAT SLOPPY TO YOU?
IT'S NOT JUST ME, YOU KNOW.

THWAP
?

!

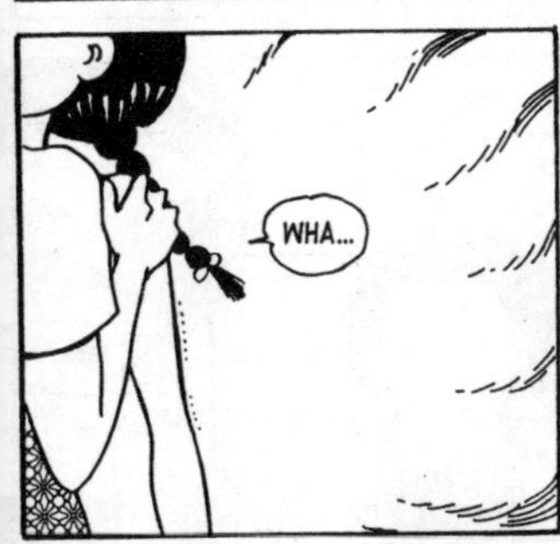
WHA...

WHAT ARE YOU DOING?!
SNAP

HOW... HOW CAN YOU...?!

KANGAE NAH! I'M GONNA MARRY YOU ONE DAY!

ACK!
SO YOU'RE ACTING LIKE A PIG BECAUSE YOU'RE A MAN, HUH? GET OUT! GET OUT!

JEEZ, HE'S GETTING WORSE...

KANGAE! WHY IS DAOON LEAVING IN SUCH A HURRY?

HE'S GOING HOME... SEEMS LIKE IT'S AN EMERGENCY... YOU'RE EARLY TODAY.
THEY HAD A COMPANY DINNER THING, BUT I JUST CAME HOME.

WHAT'S WRONG WITH YOUR FACE?
......

MOM? DID SOMETHING HAPPEN AGAIN?

YOU DON'T NEED TO WORRY ABOUT IT...

IT'S WORK-RELATED...

!

WAHHHHH~

KANGAE...
SNIFF
POUT

OOHHHHH...
WERE YOU... FIRED?

SHAKE
SHAKE

THEN DID THAT DIRECTOR LADY OR SOMETHING GET MAD AT YOU AGAIN?

NOD
NOD

WHAT'S THAT WOMAN'S PROBLEM?
SHE THINKS YOU'RE STUPID OR SOMETHING, HUH?

YOU WANT ME TO GO OVER THERE AND BEAT HER UP?
HUH?

NO, KANGAE! WHAT IF...

I GET FIRED FOR THAT?

SEEMED LIKE SHE WAS FRIENDS WITH THE PRESIDENT OF THE COMPANY, TOO.
MOM-. WHAT ARE YOU SO AFRAID OF? IF YOU GET FIRED, YOU GET FIRED.

THEN HOW DO WE LIVE?
JUST SELL THIS HOUSE AND MOVE INTO A SMALLER PLACE...

NO WAY!
EEP!
BOLT

YOUR FATHER SPENT HIS ENTIRE LIFE BUILDING THIS HOUSE!

Z

DING DONG

WHO'S THAT?
IGNORE IT AND KEEP GOING!

AMI... IT'S ME! THE DOOR'S UNLOCKED...

!

KANGAE!

!!

HEY! YOU, YOU DIDN'T LOCK THE DOOR?
I WAS IN A HURRY, SO...

YOU IDIOT!
WHAP

AMI...AMI...
......

I...I DO'N...T WANT TO BE AN ADULT.

# the great CATSBY

*by Doha*

Catsby, a twenty-something nobody, loses his girl-friend to another man... A richer man. His pal Houndu treats him to wine, women and song, but there's no forgetting his lost Persu. The thousand humiliations of youth are poured upon Catsby, who feels far too much to begin with, and whose prospects go from bad to worse. Now he's petrified of his father, now drunk on the floor, now freaking over a blind-date, now convinced it's all for nothing. No detail however vulgar or delicate is left out as the angst of youth is beautifully dissected.

- **Drama for Age 16+**

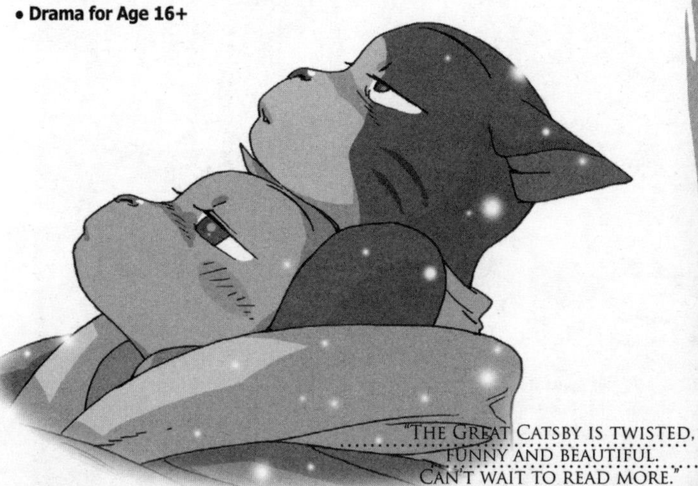

"THE GREAT CATSBY IS TWISTED, FUNNY AND BEAUTIFUL. CAN'T WAIT TO READ MORE."

*- Scott McCloud, Author, Understanding Comics*

STUMP
STUMP
THE NAME'S CATSBY..
TWENTY-SIX-YEAR-OLD MALE..
A TOTAL BUM WITH NO AMBITIONS..
ARE DESCRIPTIONS THAT APTLY DEFINE ME.
PASS THE NEIGHBORHOOD SCHEDULED FOR FORCED EVACUATION..
PASS THE STATE EXAM PREPARERS' NEIGHBORHOOD..
DOWN THE SKYWARD ALLEY..
AND ARRIVE AT ANOTHER NEIGHBORHOOD SET FOR FORCED EVACUATION.
NOT SMART, BUT SUCH A PATH SERVES AS A SHORTCUT..

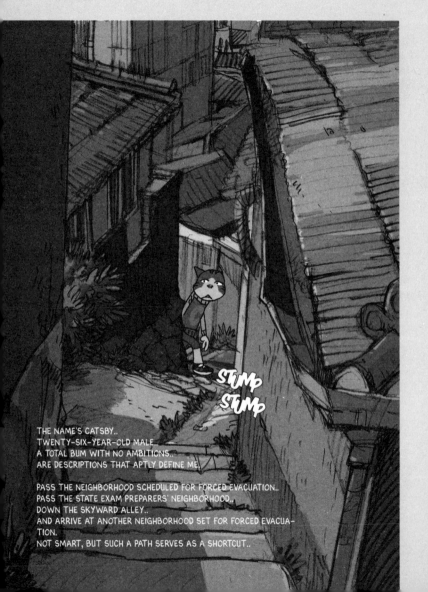

I LIVE IN A "PENTHOUSE."

FOR A MALE WHO HAS KEPT CLEAR OF PRESTIGIOUS SCHOOLS
AND MAJORS WITH A FUTURE, THE RIGHT TO CHOOSE HIS JOB
IS IMPERTINENT GREED TO BEGIN WITH..
THE NOTION THAT I'M NOT THE ONLY ONE SERVES AS A COMFORT...?

ONLY RUBBER..
THIS PETTY THING!
RUBBER..

SWEAT SO THAT LIFE DOESN'T BECOME DRY..
THE SIGNIFICANCE OF SWEAT.. NEED I REPEAT??

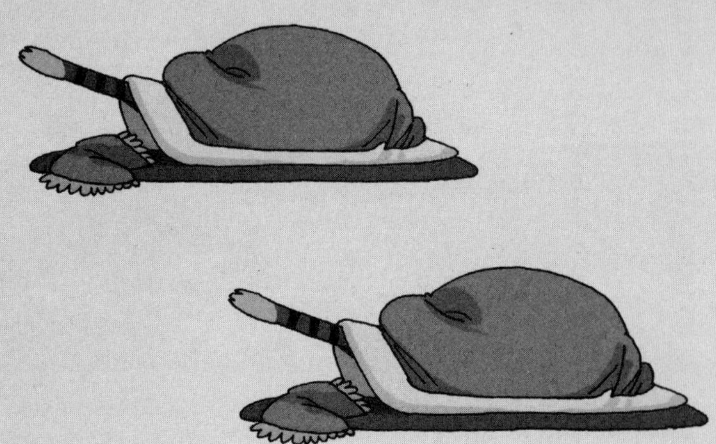

CAN YOU GET OFF?

I... I... I'M STILL IN THE "EJECT" MODE...

FIPP

MY WOMAN.. PERSU
AT HEART.. I BELIEVE HER TO BE AN "OASIS"..

YOU SMOKE?
SINCE... WHEN?

PUFFFFFF~

DECIDED TO START..

SIXTH YEAR..
A FRIEND I TUMBLE WITH WITHOUT MUCH PROBLEM, WHO I ENJOY TILL I'M NOT THIRSTY. DID SHE COME WITH HER MIND SET? SHE'S.. FEROCIOUSLY.. ON EDGE.

NICE WEATHER~
ISN'T IT A SIN TO TUMBLE
IN A BACK ROOM AT THIS HOUR?

SHOULD WE GO OUT
FOR A WALK?

LOOK AT THE CLOCK...

RIGHT!!
TIME FOR HOUNDU'S RETURN...

MY COLLEGE CLASSMATE HOUNDU IS THE REAL OWNER OF THIS "PENTHOUSE."
HOMIE RETURNS HOME LATE FOR ME WHEN PERSU COMES BY.

I DON'T SIT AROUND
LIKE AN IDIOT...
TEATIME OMITTED.

THERE'S NOTHING WRONG
WITH BEFRIENDING
A CONDOM, RIGHT?

IT'S ONLY RUBBER... RUBBER...
USING IT ALL OF A SUDDEN,
I CAN'T GET A FEEL...

WOMEN WANT IT.

RIGHT...
IT'S NOT THAT I DON'T KNOW!!
JUST THAT HAVING SOMETHING
THRUST ITSELF BETWEEN US...

**OH! MY! GOD!!**

A GIFT.. NOT EVEN ON A SPECIAL DAY..
AM ALREADY THANKFUL FOR HELPING
MY LIFE NOT BE DRY...
MOVED.. AGAIN..

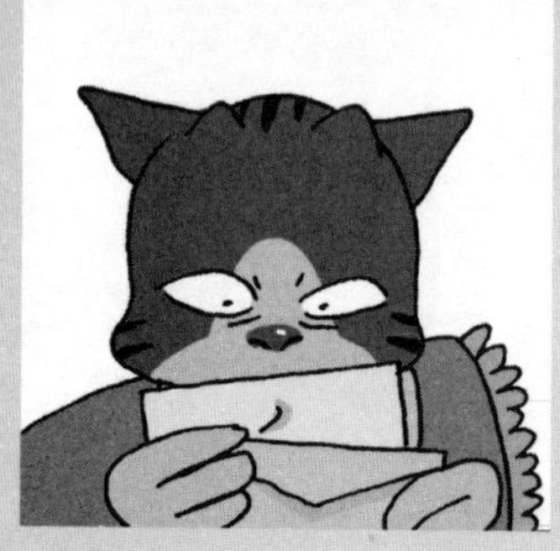

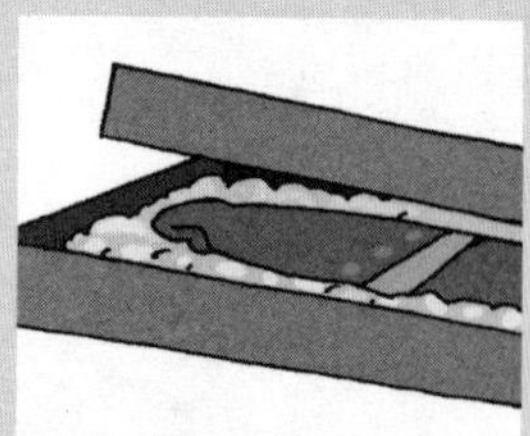

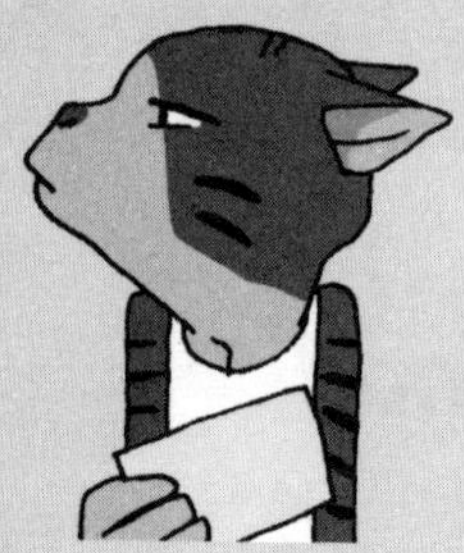

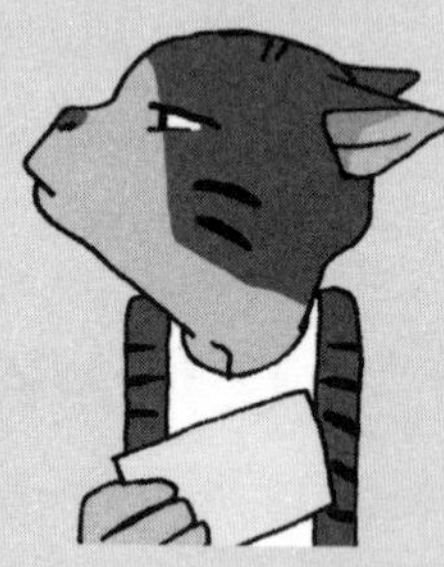

TAKE BACK
BEING MOVED.

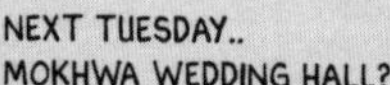
NEXT TUESDAY..
MOKHWA WEDDING HALL?

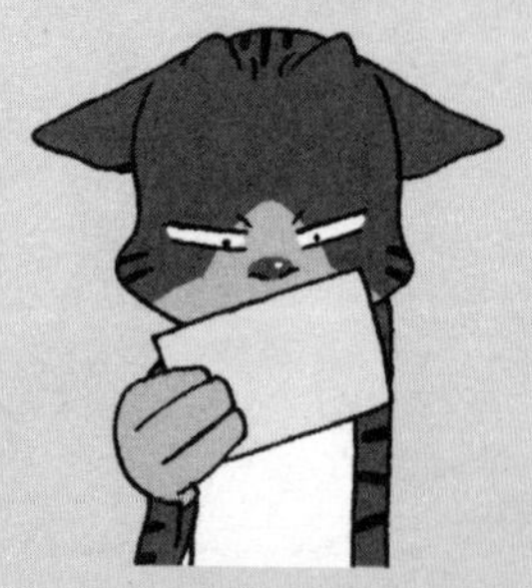

THREE DAYS TO THE WEDDING
OF A WOMAN I DATED FOR SIX YEARS.

AS MANY AS...
72 LONG HOURS.. LEFT.
2,160 MINUTES..
129,600 SECONDS..

THE CALCULATION'S SPEEDING UP BY ITSELF..
MY SLOW BRAIN'S MOVING FAST..
NO.. 129,599 SECONDS
129,598..

HOUNDU IS
A COLLEGE CLASSMATE.

LANDS A JOB AT A COMPANY UPON GRADUATION,
SPENDS TWO YEARS BORED,
THEN GIVES UP THE BADGE
OF AN ASSISTANT MANAGER POSITION.

NOW, UTILIZING HIS FRIENDLY NATURE
AND KEY TALENT..
HE'S A RISING STAR IN THE KANGNAM*
PRIVATE TUTORING MARKET.

HE'D RATHER BE CALLED "THE RISING STAR"
THAN HOUNDU..

WHAT DOES HE FORSAKE AND COVET...
THOUGH IT'S AN IMPROPER NICKNAME
HE HIMSELF CHOSE..

*KANGNAM: DOWNTOWN SEOUL BELOW HAN RIVER

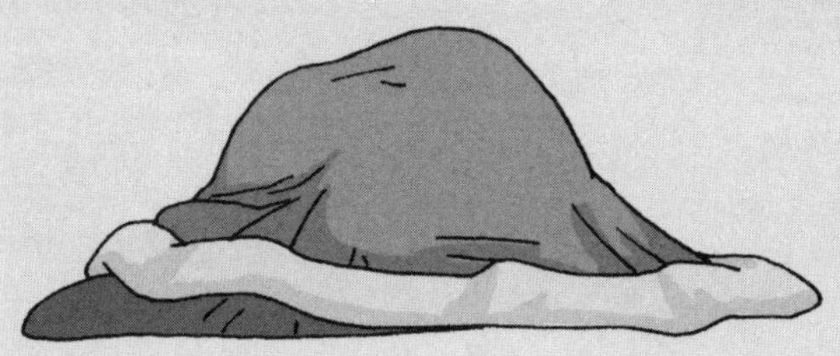

IF ONE OF US DIES EATING,
THERE'LL BE ENOUGH OF *MY AUNTIE'S PIG FEET*
LEFT TO POP THE OTHER'S STOMACH!!

PERFUME'S...
LOLITA LEMPICKA?

DOG-NOSED.. HOUNDU

PERSU CAME BY.
MOVE IN TOGETHER. WHY DON'T YOU!! YOU'RE GONNA BUY THAT COMFORTER. RIGHT? THINK THIS IS SOME KIND OF MOTEL OR SOMETHING!!

SHE LEFT...
SIP
.......

IT'S DIFFICULT TO THROW UP
SIX YEAR'S DATING GAME
WITH A BOTTLE OF SOJU*..
NO.. NOT ONLY WAS IT IMPOSSIBLE,
BUT THERE WAS NEITHER
A MEANING NOR A REASON FOR IT..

WHY DIDN'T YOU STOP HER...

DUDE WHO KNOWS THE ANSWER
EVEN WHEN HE DOESN'T GET
AN ANSWER.

*SOJU : KOREA'S MOST COMMON, INEXPENSIVE SPIRIT.

THE REASON PERSU LEFT..

THE REASON I COULDN'T STOP HER..

WOULD HE HAVE A HOUSE, CAR, AND POWER?!! HE'S PROBABLY A REAL HAPPENING PRICK, RIGHT?? YOU KNOW HOW CRAZY PARTICULAR!! PERSU... IS...

OF COURSE... HE WOULD, RIGHT?? WHO DOESN'T HAVE THAT MUCH... NOWADAYS... EXCEPT YOU...

HA-HA-HA

WATCHING YOU SMILE BOOSTS MY APPETITE FOR DRINKING...

SO... JU... SHOULD I GET... SOME MO... MORE? SHOULD... DRINK WHEN YOU HAVE AN APPETITE!!

KEEP THAT FACE.

SWASHHHHHHHHHHH

PLOOP

PLOOP

PLOOP

PLOOP

PLOOP

PLOOP

PLOOP

PLOOP

PLOOP

IT'S NOT..
ENTIRELY WRONG..

WHAT HOUNDU SAID.

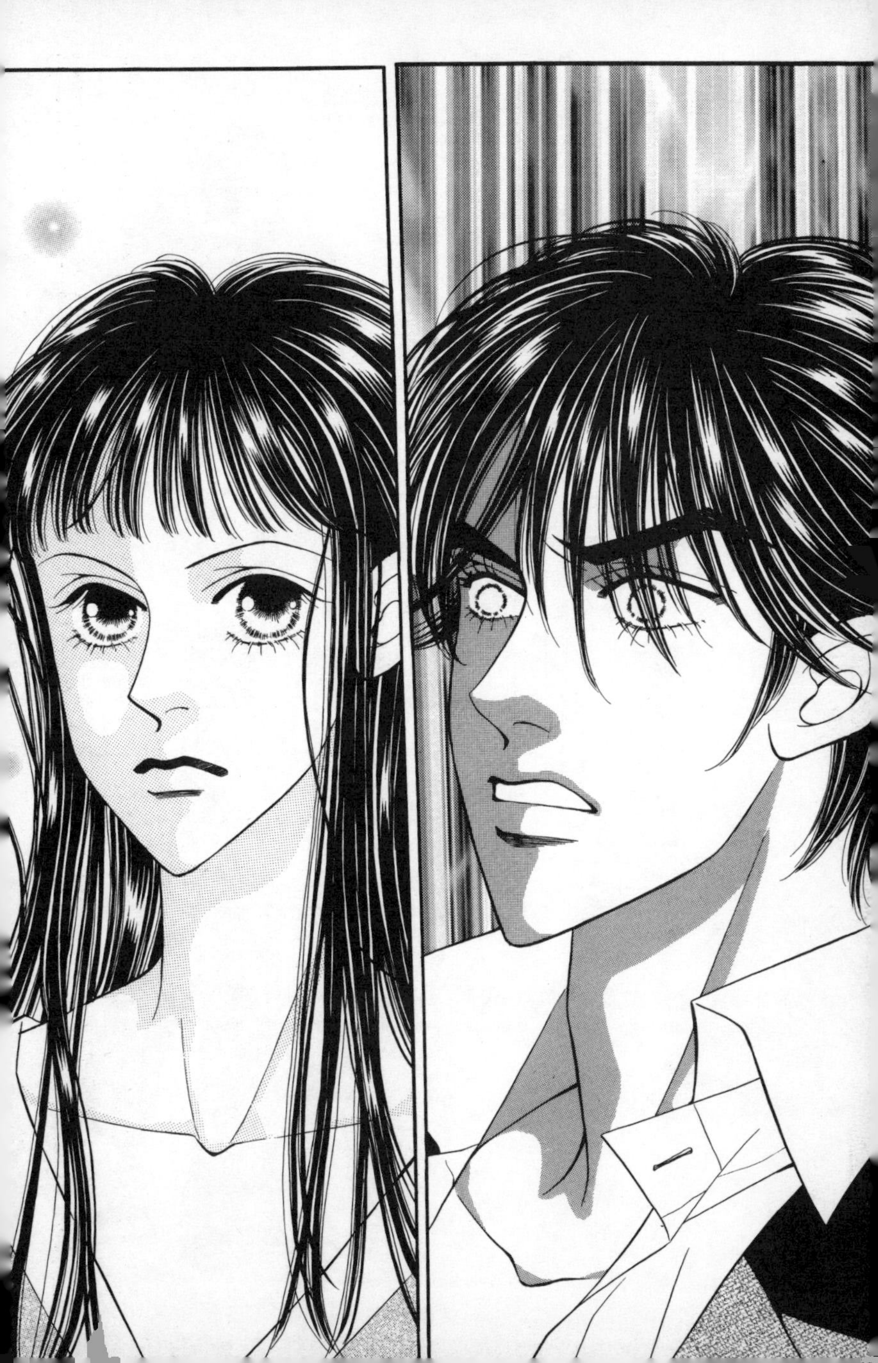

WHAT THE HELL
IS THIS~!!

YOU TOOK S4 OUT OF THE BASEMENT~?!
HAVE YOU FORGOTTEN THE RULES?
UNDER NO CIRCUMSTANCES CAN HUMAN CLONES LEAVE THE BASEMENT LAB~~!!
...
JAEHEE ISN'T HERE ANYMORE- BUT S4
IS THE ONLY LIVING BEING
THAT HAS JAEHEE'S DNA.
WE WILL REGISTER S4 AS PROFESSOR PILYONG SUH'S
SECOND OLDEST DAUGHTER.
NOTHING CAN JUSTIFY WHAT YOU DID~!!
...

AND WE WILL BE HER LEGAL GUARDIANS.
JUST AS WITH NARI SONG, THE FIRST SPARE CLONE!
...YOU ARE OUT OF YOUR MIND...!
COMPLETELY MAD...!
WE'RE CALLING OFF ALL THE HUMAN CLONE PROJECTS.
S1 IS OUT OF OUR HANDS BECAUSE DR. SONG ALREADY REGISTERED HER AS HIS OWN,
BUT S4 WILL BE DESTROYED ALONG WITH THE BASEMENT LAB!

SHE'S JAEHEE'S CLONE. HOW CAN YOU DO SUCH A THING~~?!
DON'T DRAG JAEHEE INTO THIS~!!
NOTHING CAN EVER REPLACE JAEHEE~~!
WHAT'S MORE APPALLING IS THAT JAEHEE-LIKE THING
WANDERING BEFORE MY EYES~!!
NO~!! I WON'T AGREE!!
I DON'T NEED YOUR PATHETIC APPROVAL!
BECAUSE I HAVE THE AUTHORITY TO MAKE ALL DECISIONS~!

FROM NOW ON, YOU'RE NOT ALLOWED TO DO WHATEVER YOU WANT~!!

SLAM

THAT JERK...

SWIRP
SNATCH
WHEEE

WHUMP
THUD
THUMP
THUMP
TUMBLE
TUMBLE
JUST REMEMBER THAT THE DAY YOU TRY TO CRAWL OUT OF THERE
IS THE DAY YOU'RE GOING TO DIE.
COOM...

I CAN'T CRY, JAEHEE...
EVEN IF MY BODY IS TORN INTO PIECES...
BECAUSE I WILL NEVER FORGIVE MYSELF...
MR. GANGJAE LEE?

I'M DOEHYUN DOE FROM THE SUPREME PROSECUTOR'S
OFFICE IN SEOUL.
I THOUGHT WE NOTIFIED YOU ABOUT INTERVIEWING THE WITNESSES TODAY.
YOU SHOULDN'T BE IGNORING US LIKE THIS.

BECAUSE YOU ARE
THE LEADING SUSPECT IN THIS CASE.

## Manhwa Novella Collection Vol. 1: Lie to Me

*by Youngran Lee*

NETCOMICS presents Manhwa Novella Collection—an anthology of shorter works from the most prominent Korean comic authors! Volume 1 of this sensational series contains three popular shorter works by one of the most famous shojo writers in Korea.

## Manhwa Novella Collection Vol. 2: 9 Faces of Love

*by Wann*

Volume 2 of this sensational, new series contains nine of the most popular shorter works by Wann, the author of *Can't Lose You.* Wann's colorful vignettes depict the most vexing of human emotions, love, in all its guises.

## Manhwa Novella Collection Vol. 3: The Starry Night

*by Kimjin*

Featuring four gripping tales that mix and match genres with gleeful abandon, the third volume of NETCOMICS Manhwa Novella Collection will touch your heart, mind, and funny bone all at once!

## Manhwa Novella Collection Vol. 4: The Devil's Trill

*by Sooyeon Won*

The fourth volume features two classic, gothic stories of vampiric love and professional obsession by the creator of the smash-hit *Let Dai* Sooyeon Won.

**Available now at your favorite bookstores.**
**Read them online at www.NETCOMICS.com!**

# in the STARLIGHT

by Kyungok Kang

Shinhye loves lying under the night sky with her father, listening to his tales of the constellations. And she dreams of a life among the stars. Little does she know that the stars may come down to her instead. Her journey begins when the Department of Science asks her family to host Sarah, a foreign girl with a unique talent. But, strange men are interested in Sarah and Shinhye doesn't know why. Unbeknownst to Shinhye, her every dream-and nightmare-is about to come true.

- **SF/Fantasy for Age 13+**



"I'M SURE THERE'S A LOT OF SORROWS, SUFFERING, AND A GREATER SURPRISE IN STORE, BUT I BET THE EMOTIONAL TURMOILS WILL BALANCE WITH A WHOLESOME AND SATISFYING ENDING..."

*– Patty Loi, NETCOMICS subscriber*

KA...
SIRA...
WHAT'S... THAT SOUND? "KA... SIRA...
THUD.. THUD.. THUD..
AND THIS... VIBRATION...?
IT SOUNDS LIKE A HEARTBEAT... FOR SOME REASON...

HUH...?
RRUMBLE...
KRAACK
EARTHQUAKE!
EEP!
IT STOPPED?
......?
SOMETHING'S DOWN THERE... BETWEEN THOSE CRACKS!

KHAKK----!

HUKK!
THAT DREAM... AGAIN...
I THOUGHT
IT WENT AWAY
A FEW MONTHS AGO...
BUT IT CAME BACK...
FOR WHAT POSSIBLE
REASON DO I KEEP
HAVING THIS DREAM?
BOY...
FATHER FELL
ASLEEP TODAY,
TOO.

THE STARS ARE
FLOWING....

BRRINNGG....
BRRIIINNGG....
YAY~, I FEEL GREAT. THE WEATHER'S BEEN SO NICE LATELY, AUNTIE-.
DID WE GET THE NEWSPAPER?
YES.
AND THE MILK?
I GOT IT.
...HUH?
THERE'S BEEN ANOTHER UFO SIGHTING IN AMERICA, AUNTIE.
ARE THE ALIENS GOING THERE TO WATCH "E.T." SINCE IT'S PRODUCED THERE OR SOMETHING?
HOW COME THEY DON'T SHOW UP IN KOREA, BUT ALWAYS IN AMERICA?
THIS IS DISCRIMI-NATION!
LOOK! AGAIN IN THE NEWSPAPER TWO WEEKS AGO...
ANYWAY, GO WAKE YOUR FATHER UP.
OH~, AND SHINHYE?
WOW-!, 7 O'CLOCK ALREADY...
OH YEAH, RIGHT!
HE SAID HE WAS LEAVING EARLY TODAY!

YEAH?
WHAT IS IT, AUNTIE?
THAT PTA MEETING WE TALKED ABOUT LAST TIME... I DECIDED TO GO BECAUSE YOUR FATHER IS BUSY AS ALWAYS.
OKAY.
SHE'S GROWN SO MUCH...
17 YEARS OLD ALREADY...
SHE JUST ADORES HER FATHER...

HELLO!
HI!
HEY, DID YOU SEE THE "SURPRISE SHOW" LAST NIGHT?
HUH?! OH YEAH... THE ONE WHERE SOMEONE BROKE A CHOPSTICK WITH HIS EYES?
GOSH, IF SOMETHING LIKE THAT HAPPENED IN FRONT OF ME, I'D FREAK OUT!
WHAT DO YOU THINK, SHINHYE?
UNLESS WE'RE DIRECTLY INVOLVED. I GUESS WE'LL NEVER KNOW.
WHY? WE HEAR ABOUT IT A LOT. I THINK PSYCHIC POWERS LIKE "ESP" HAVE SOME TRUTH TO THEM!
EVEN IF STUFF LIKE THAT HAPPENED RIGHT BEFORE YOUR EYES, IT'D STILL BE HARD TO BELIEVE.
I DON'T BELIEVE IN STUFF LIKE THAT. IT'S GOTTA BE A TRICK!
BUT, I DO BELIEVE IN THE EXISTENCE OF SUCH ABILITIES.
I KINDA THINK IT'S POSSIBLE, BUT SINCE I DON'T HAVE ESP...
IT'S HARD FOR ME TO COMPLETELY TRUST IN SOMEONE ELSE'S ABILITY!

YOU CAN DO COOL STUFF WITH IT, BUT YOU'LL BE TREATED LIKE A MONSTER OR A MONKEY AT THE ZOO.
YEAH, IT'S NOT A COMMON ABILITY...
MAYBE IT'S JEALOUSY OF SOME KIND... WE'RE JEALOUS BECAUSE THAT PERSON CAN DO WHAT YOU AND I CAN'T DO, YOU KNOW?!
ESP DOESN'T HAPPEN JUST BECAUSE YOU WANT IT. IT'S AN ABILITY YOU'RE BORN WITH!
EVEN THOUGH THEY MAY BE BORN WAY BEFORE THEIR TIME...
EVEN THOUGH THEY MAY NOT BE IN TUNE WITH REALITY...
WHY DOES IT HAVE TO BE THAT WAY?
I DON'T LIKE THAT!
THAT'S TRUE, BUT HONESTLY...
I THINK THEY CAME INTO THIS WORLD BECAUSE WE NEED THEM RIGHT NOW IN THIS ERA!
THEIR POWERS ALONE MUST BE A BURDEN TO THEM, BUT WE'RE MAKING IT INTO A FREAK SHOW!

IT'S UNREALISTIC FOR THAT PERSON TO AVOID BEING A FREAK SHOW. IF SOMEONE WITH ESP WAS SITTING BESIDE YOU, WOULDN'T YOU WANT TO STARE?
ANYONE WHO'S A NOVELTY IS ALREADY A SIDE SHOW. WHO WOULDN'T WANT TO SEE AN ALIEN THAT JUST APPEARED?
IN OTHER WORDS, ALTHOUGH THAT PERSON DOESN'T WANT TO BE A CIRCUS FREAK,
HE OR SHE IS AN ALIEN AND THEREFORE, IS ALREADY A SHOW CASE.
THAT'S TRUE, YOU'RE RIGHT...
BUT EVEN THOUGH EVERYONE LOOKS, I THINK IT STILL MATTERS HOW WE LOOK AT THE PERSON.
DON'T YOU EVER THINK ABOUT HOW WE MAKE THAT ALIEN FEEL?

DING DONG
MORNING ROLL CALL.
HOW DID THE DISCUSSION GET ALL SO GRANDIOSE?
IT'S SHINHYE'S FAULT. WHENEVER WE TALK TO HER, THE TOPIC GETS SO SERIOUS!
I UNDERSTAND SHE'S BEING OPEN, BUT...

DING DONG

LET'S GO TO THE DDUKBOKKI* JOINT!

MEOW?

THE TICKET TO DDUKBOKKI HEAVEN?

*SNIFF* MY KID SISTER TOLD ME TO WASH HER SCHOOL SLIPPERS.

SHE'S JEALOUS THAT WE DON'T HAVE TO WEAR 'EM.

THERE ARE MORE GIRLS THAN GUYS...

WHY IS THAT?

AND YOU LEFT YOUR SISTER ALONE?

WE WEAR UNIFORMS INSTEAD!

WHAT ABOUT "BACK TO THE FUTURE"?

HAVE YOU SEEN THE MOVIE "TWO WILL COME"?

OH! WHEN DID IT COME OUT?

WHAT ABOUT "NARRATION OF LOVE AT 17"?

CRA-ZY

*DDUKBOKKI: A BROILED DISH OF RICE CAKE IN SPICY PEPPER SAUCE

I DIDN'T KNOW YOU RODE A BIKE TO SCHOOL
...
I USUALLY DO, BUT I WASN'T ABLE TO FOR THE PAST FEW DAYS BECAUSE I WAS GETTING IT FIXED.
WANT A RIDE? I PROMISE NOT TO KILL YOU.
YUP!
...
YOU REALLY THINK SO?
THINK WHAT?
I MEAN THE SPECIAL PEOPLE--NOT CONSIDERING PEOPLE WITH ESP AS FREAKS...
WELL, MAYBE THE FIRST TIME I MEET THEM.
AFTER ALL, I'VE NEVER SEEN THEM BEFORE.
BUT, I DON'T WANNA LOOK AT THEM IN THAT SORT OF WAY!
I SEEM TO RUN INTO THAT TOPIC A LOT TODAY!
YEAH...

LET'S GO.
SUH
WOW~, IT'S HUGE!
DONGHOON, YOU'RE HOME.
HELLO, UNCLE. YOU HEADING OUT?
UM~, THIS IS MY FRIEND. SHE CAME TO SEE THE FILM...
AH, HELLO. WELCOME. YOU'RE MISS SHINHYE YOO.
PLEASED TO MEET YOU.
OH! YOU KNOW MY NAME.
HAHA~. IT'S BECAUSE DONG-HOON...
WEREN'T YOU IN A HURRY, UNCLE? GOOD BYE!

HAHA~.
OKAY, I'M OFF.
HAVE FUN,
SHINHYE.
THANK YOU, I WILL.
OH, YEAH!
SORRY, CAN YOU GO INSIDE FIRST, SHINHYE?
IT'LL BE QUICK-.
I NEED TO TALK TO MY UNCLE ABOUT SOMETHING.
OKAY.
MA'AM, CAN YOU GIVE HER SOMETHING TO DRINK?
OH, YOU'RE HOME.
YOU BROUGHT A GIRLFRIEND TODAY~.
HELLO.
ALRIGHT THEN.
?
UNCLE ---.

THAT THING YOU WERE TALKING ABOUT YESTERDAY... IT'S NOT RESOLVED YET, IS IT?
NO. THE ISSUE WILL BE DECIDED TODAY, BUT I EXPECT THE HOUSE WILL BE OURS...
UM, ACTUALLY... THAT GIRL JUST NOW...!
THIS IS GOOD. HOW DO THEY MAKE THIS?
SHOULD I TRY TO MAKE IT FOR DAD?
MAYBE AUNTIE KNOWS HOW...
SHINHYE-.
DONG-HOON...
AH-.
NO, BE AT EASE! PLEASE SIT DOWN.
ACTUALLY, I CAME BACK BECAUSE I HAVE SOMETHING TO SAY TO YOU.

SO YOUR FATHER'S AN ASTRONOMY PROFESSOR?

YES.

AND UH... YOU'RE QUITE INTERESTED IN SCIENCE?

YES... A LITTLE...

AND... UM... DONGHOON TELLS ME YOU'RE NOT BIASED AGAINST PEOPLE WITH ESP, IS THAT RIGHT?

YES.

AND YOU HAVE THREE PEOPLE IN YOUR FAMILY...

...YES...

DON'T FEEL OFFENDED BY ALL THE QUESTIONS.

IF IT'S ALL RIGHT, CAN WE HAVE SOMEONE STAY AT YOUR PLACE FOR 2 MONTHS?

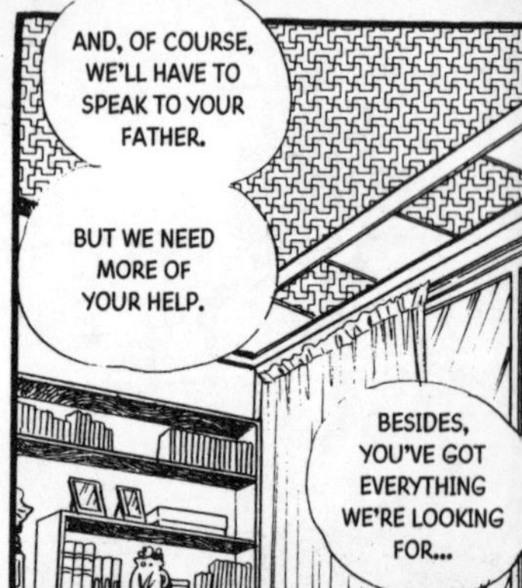

AND, OF COURSE, WE'LL HAVE TO SPEAK TO YOUR FATHER.
BUT WE NEED MORE OF YOUR HELP.
BESIDES, YOU'VE GOT EVERYTHING WE'RE LOOKING FOR...

BUT, I'M CURIOUS WHY YOU NEED MY HELP. WHAT KIND OF PERSON ARE WE TALKING ABOUT?
THE HOUSE ISN'T SMALL, SO MY AUNTIE WILL PROBABLY BE ALRIGHT WITH IT, TOO...
I... I DON'T MIND AS LONG AS MY FATHER SAYS IT'S OKAY.
WELL...
YOU MAY NOT BELIEVE THIS BUT...
THIS PERSON HAS ESP.

SORRY?
SHE'S A GIRL YOUR AGE.
SHE'S FOREIGN, BUT LOOKS ASIAN BECAUSE SHE'S PARTIALLY KOREAN!
SHE'S STAYING IN KOREA BECAUSE OF EXTENUATING CIRCUMSTANCES.
HOW SHOULD I PUT IT... SHE REALLY HATES SPECIAL TREATMENT.
SHE'S ALREADY STAYED IN SEVERAL HOMES BUT LEFT BECAUSE SHE DIDN'T LIKE THEM.
"SPECIAL TREATMENT" IS A GOOD WAY TO PUT IT.
SHE HATED THEM BECAUSE THEY TREATED HER LIKE A FREAK SHOW!
SHE HATES STAYING IN HOTELS EVEN MORE.
SO, WE NEED SOMEONE WHO WON'T TREAT HER SPECIALLY AND CAN BE A FRIEND TO HER. I THINK SHE WOULD GET ALONG WITH ANOTHER GIRL HER AGE.
......
THEY DON SOUND LI THEY'RE JOKIN AT AL
UM... WELL...

See what happens next at www.NETCOMICS.com!

# Two Will Come

*by Kyungok Kang*

Ordinary high school girl Jina discovers that she is heir to a terrible legacy handed down from her family's sinister history. Long ago, her ancestors killed a magical serpent known as an Imugi, believing that it would bring them good luck. Unfortunately, the creature cursed them as it died, decreeing that one family member of each generation for that day forth will be killed by two people closely acquainted with that person. One of Jina's relatives has been murdered without fail in every generation. Now, Jina has been informed that she will be next to die. Can she possibly escape this horrid fate?

- **Mystery/Horror for Age 13+**

"THE STORY HAS AN INTERESTING PREMISE, AND THE SET UP IS SUSPENSEFUL."
– *V Reb, NETCOMICS subscriber*

IT WASN'T ME...
I... ALWAYS THOUGHT FOR CERTAIN THAT IT WAS GOING TO BE ME...
JUST THE WAY MY MOM SAID TO ME, EVER SINCE I WAS LITTLE...
THAT I SHOULD PAY FOR THE SINS...
THAT.... I.... SHOULD... DIE....
YOUR MOTHER WASN'T SANE WHEN SHE SAID THAT...
YOU KNOW SHE DIDN'T MEAN IT....
WHO DID THE FORTUNE TELLER SAY IT WAS GOING TO BE?
IT'S FROM THIS HOUSEHOLD...
THEY WON'T TELL US, BUT...
CONSIDERING THAT IT'S GOING TO BE OUR GENERATION, IT'S EITHER JINA OR JIWOO.
HEARD THEY'RE GOING TO DO AN EXORCISM.

EXORCISM?
EXORCISMS ARE VERY EXPENSIVE IN THIS COUNTRY.
AND THEY'RE GONNA DO THAT BASED ON SOME FORTUNE TELLING THAT MAY OR MAY NOT BE ACCURATE.
BUT I'M PRETTY SURE HE'S A PHONY FORTUNE TELLER.
OLD-FASHIONED GROWN-UPS ARE LIKE THAT-.
I DON'T BELIEVE IN THE PREDICTION.
BESIDES.... THE LAST INCIDENT ALSO TOOK PLACE IN THIS FAMILY.
HONEY... DON'T YOU THINK.... WE SHOULD TELL JINA ABOUT THIS?
DON'T BOTHER-. IF WE CAN PREVENT IT WITH AN EXORCISM, WE DON'T NEED TO TELL HER.
BUT...
WHAT'S WRONG WITH YOU? YOU SAID YOU DIDN'T BELIEVE IN IT!
ARE YOU GETTING SOFT AFTER HEARING WHAT THE FORTUNE TELLER SAID?

THINK ABOUT IT-. HOW CAN YOU TELL OUR DAUGHTER THAT THERE ARE 2 PEOPLE AROUND HER WHO ARE OUT TO KILL HER,
AND THAT NOBODY KNOWS WHO THEY ARE.
THAT THEY... COULD POSSIBLY BE HER BROTHER OR EVEN HER PARENTS!!
JUST LIKE WHAT HAPPENED TO MY SISTERS LAST TIME.
.... LOWER YOUR VOICE...
IF THAT PREDICTION IS CORRECT,
IF THAT SHAMAN SAW ANY TRUTH...
THEN SUCH AN EXPENSIVE EXORCISM IS OUT OF THE QUESTION.

YOU SHOULDN'T EXPECT ANY PAYBACK IN PROPER FORTUNE TELLING.
IF YOU DO, YOU'LL HAVE A HARD TIME EVEN SEEING THINGS THAT YOU WERE MEANT TO SEE.
TWO NINE TWO FIVE ONE THREE 292513
IT'S DIFFERENT FROM TELLING FORTUNES FOR FUN.
IF HE TRIES TO GET PAID FOR MORE THAN HE SAW AND CONVEYED TO HIS CLIENTS, HE'LL PAY FOR HIS ACTIONS. THE PUNISHMENT WILL FIT THE CRIME.
THAT'S A UNIVERSAL LAW AMONG TRUE PSYCHICS.
PEOPLE WHO BELIEVE IN SUCH PSYCHICS ARE IDIOTS, BUT
IF HE'S GOING TO SELL COMMERCIALIZED PSYCHIC POWERS, HE SHOULD FOOL WITH SMALLER AMOUNTS OF MONEY.
KNOCK IT OFF WITH THE COMPLICATED TALK.
THAT'S YOUR SPECIALTY, I DON'T KNOW ANYTHING ABOUT IT.
WAIT-
DID YOU... ALREADY KNOW ABOUT THIS?

A LITTLE.
THEN... IT'S REALLY GOING TO BE...
JINA-?
I'VE BEEN FEELING IT... EVER SINCE I SAW HER FOR THE FIRST TIME.
See what happens next at www.NETCOMICS.com!

# 100% Perfect Girl

© Wann / NETCOMICS

Jay Jinn is the headstrong teenage rebel, determined to prove she's serious about making art. J. Max is the tall debonair foreigner, in Korea on business, with more to his background than he lets on. On the surface, it would seem as though Jay and J. have nothing in common... until a chance encounter in a hotel lobby sparks a mysterious attraction. A giddy romantic fable for our ever-shrinking world, *100% Perfect Girl* demonstrates the power of chemistry to conquer all.

- **Romance/Fantasy for Age 13+**

"WHAT A BEAUTIFUL PIECE OF WORK THIS IS! THE ART IS GORGEOUS AND THE STORY IS CAPTIVATING."

*– Jenny Kelzenberg, NETCOMICS subscriber*

WHAT?
ADVICE CENTER
SOHYUN IS GOING TO REPRESENT OUR SCHOOL?
BUT I'M THE ONE WHO WON THE SCHOOL CONTEST!
THAT'S TRUE-.
BUT SOHYUN IS PLANNING TO STUDY ABROAD AFTER GRADUATION.
IT SEEMS AS IF WINNING A PRIZE FOR THE UPCOMING FINE ART COMPETITION IS IMPORTANT FOR HER FUTURE.
SO YOU SHOULD CONCEDE.
THE COLLEGE ENTRANCE EXAM ISN'T FAR AWAY, AND YOU'RE NOT APPLYING TO AN ART SCHOOL ANYWAY.
CLICK

THAT'S NOT RIGHT! HOW CAN THEY DO THAT?
SHE SPENT TONS OF MONEY ON PRIVATE LESSONS FROM ART PROFESSORS, AND STUFF LIKE THAT... HA!
WHAT, YOU'RE NOT UPSET?
YOU WERE LOOKING FORWARD TO IT
IT'S OKAY.
ANYWAY... I CAN ONLY PAINT AS A HOBBY.
HALT...
IT'S... NOT.... OKAY.

HI, JAY.
HI, NOLAN
JIN'S HOMESTAY
CAN YOU TELL YOUR MOTHER THAT I WON'T BE IN FOR DINNER? I'M GOING TO A PARTY TONIGHT.
NOLAN, AREN'T YOU PARTYING TOO MUCH?
HAHA, LET ME OFF THE HOOK THIS TIME. IT'S A FAREWELL GATHERING FOR A FRIEND WHO'S GOING BACK HOME.
RATTLE
RATTLE
RATTLE
THE ONION...
UM, MOM...
IT'S ABOUT THE FINE ART COMPETITION ....

WHY DIDN'T YOU COME STRAIGHT HOME AFTER SCHOOL? YOU'RE LATE!
GO TO THE BARITT HOTEL- HURRY UP!
THE NEW BOARDER, FROM BOSTON OR SOMEPLACE--HE SAYS HE'S AT THE HOTEL BECAUSE HE DOESN'T KNOW THE AREA. GO AND PICK HIM UP.
M... MOM.... YOU KNOW, THE TEACHER...
WELL, MOVE IT!
CHOP
CHOP
WHAT ARE YOU BOTHERING HIM FOR? HE'S A GUY.
BESIDES, HE SAID HE'S BUSY WRITING UP A SCHOOL REPORT.
CHOP
WHAT ABOUT MY BROTHER? IT LOOKS LIKE HE'S HOME.
WHAT~? ART? WITH OUR INCOME? THAT'S ONLY FOR DAUGHTERS OF RICH PEOPLE.
HOW CAN YOU MAKE A LIVING DOING ART? YOU'RE JUST GOING TO STARVE TO DEATH!

WE NEED TO START SAVING MONEY IF WE'RE GOING TO HELP YOUR BROTHER OPEN UP A CLINIC AFTER HE GETS OUT OF MED SCHOOL.

JUST GO TO A COMMUNITY COLLEGE AND FIND A JOB. I'M SURE YOU'LL BENEFIT FROM YOUR BROTHER'S BRIGHT FUTURE.

IT'S NOT OKAY....
IT'S NOT OKAY....!
SO WHAT IF HE'S MY OLDER BROTHER? SO WHAT IF HE'S A GUY?
AND SO WHAT IF HE'S IN MEDICAL SCHOOL?
SLAM
SLIDE
WHO WAS THAT?

VIXEN.
IT'S A DECENT LOCATION.
THE BUILDING AND THE FRAMEWORK ARE GOOD. A FEW REPAIRS WOULDN'T HURT.
THE CONTRACT SIGNING FOR OUR PURCHASE OF THIS PLACE IS TOMORROW. I WAS WONDERING WHY YOU WANTED TO COME A DAY EARLY.
I SEE THAT YOU WERE PLANNING TO ASSESS THE SITUATION BEFOREHAND.
IT'S OUR FIRST TIME DIVING INTO THE KOREAN MARKET. WE SHOULDN'T BE SLACKING OFF.

...BESIDES, WHAT IF PEOPLE FOUND OUT THAT I WAS COMING?
THE MEDIA WOULD HAVE HAD A FIELD DAY AT THE AIRPORT.
YOU KNOW HOW MUCH I HATE CAMERAS AND JOURNALISTS.
OH, YES... I SEE.
BUT HAVING KAIREN WAIT OUTSIDE IS A BIT...
MIGHT BE DANGEROUS
I CAME TO LOOK IN PRIVATE. I CAN'T GO PARADING AROUND WITH BODYGUARDS ALL AROUND ME.
AND KAIREN HAS A NASTY EXPRESSION.
THERE ARE A LOT OF FOREIGNERS HERE.
I WON'T STAND OUT.
DOES HE.... REALLY THINK HE'S NOT STANDING OUT IN ANY WAY?
WHISPER
WHISPER
HE'S A MOVIE STAR, A MOVIE STAR, I TELL YOU.
NO, THAT GUY'S A MODEL.
HE DOES LOOK FAMILIAR, THOUGH...

LOOKS CLOSER TO 6' 3".
LOOK HOW TALL HE IS. HE'S DEFINITELY OVER 6 FEET.
THAT NOSE, THOSE LASHES...
HE'S REALLY HANDSOME.
ANYWAY,
A TALL MAN WHO LOOKS GOOD IN A BLACK SUIT, REALLY THAT'S...

...SEXY...!

WHAT?

WELL, THAT STUDENT GOT TIRED OF WAITING, SO HE TOOK A TAXI HERE.

HURRY HOME. YOU KNOW WE'RE MAKING SIDE DISHES TODAY, RIGHT?

GET HERE AND TRIM THE ANCHOVIES, THE RADISH TOO...

I'M NOT GOING!

WHAT?
I'M NOT GOING HOME! I'VE GOT THINGS TO DO, TOO!

I REBELLED....

THE WORLD-FAMOUS ROINNE HOTELS ARE FINALLY MAKING IT INTO KOREA. THIS IS RIDICULOUS.

WELL, WE HAD A LOT OF UNFORESEEN PROBLEMS ALONG THE WAY. FROM NOW ON, WE'LL...

UGH!

WHEW-

JAY JINN, YOUR LIFE IS ONE LONG, ROUGH ROAD.

SHOULD I...

GO FOR A WALK.

I.. I THINK THE FOOD WE HAD ON THE PLANE WASN'T FRESH.

W, WAIT FOR ME. I'LL BE BACK IN A MINUTE!

SUCH A WEAKLING.
CAN'T BELIEVE HE HAS 3 Ph.D DEGREES.

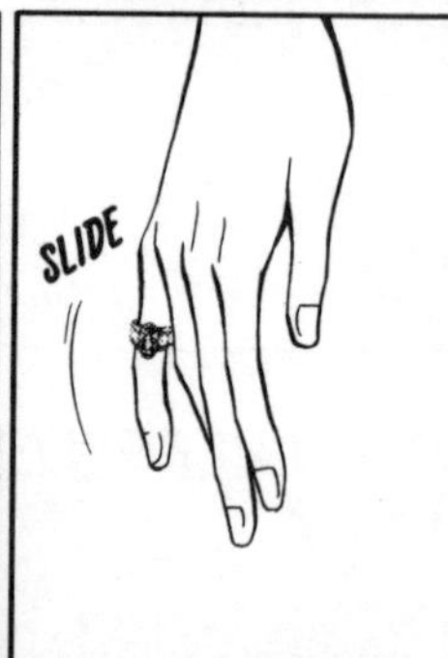

SLIDE

CLINK

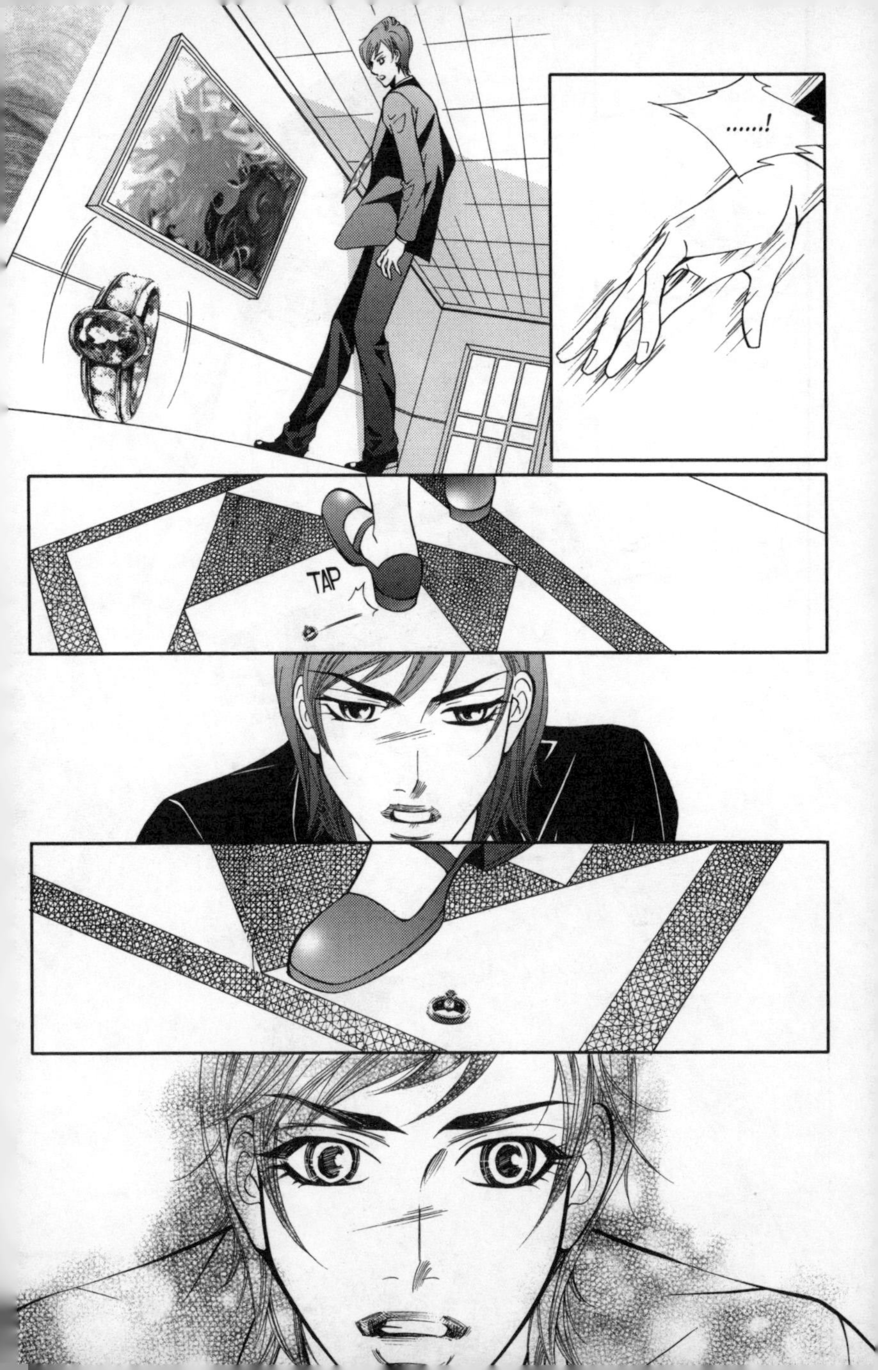
......!
TAP

See what happens next at www.NETCOMICS.com!

# CAN'T LOSE YOU

*by Wann*

In a whirlwind narrative of vanity and conceit, *Can't Lose You* is the story of two characters who come from opposite worlds but are united by the most unlikely of circumstances: Yooi is a desperate girl working day and night to earn pennies in hopes of one day paying off her father's debts and reuniting their family. Lida comes from privilege and excess, the heiress to an unbelievable fortune and a marriage match she cannot wait to consummate. But when the two girls meet and discover the one thing they have in common is their identical faces their lives take an unexpected turn.

- **Drama/Romance for Age 13+**

"A MODERN FAIRYTALE VERSION OF CINDERELLA... TOLD IN A COMPLICATED NARRATIVE INTERWEAVING COMEDY AND ACTION... WITH ART AND NARRATIVE THAT ARE SUPERB."

*- Manganews.net*

# Your Lover

by Seungwon Han

Celebrating the intricate spirit of European-style romance comes *Your Lover*, a quintessential romance story from the most-beloved Korean romance artist of our generation, Seungwon Han. Paying homage to the real-life tragic passion between Parisian painter Marie Laurencin and the famous French poet Guillaume Apollinaire, *Your Lover* paints an elaborate portrait of heart-breaks, unforgettable past experiences and unrealized dreams.

Marie loves her fiancé Woobin dearly, but Woobin dies in a tragic accident and Marie must rebuild her shattered life with Woobin's family.

There exists only one problem: Woobin's younger brother Gangbin looks exactly like him.

- **Romance/Drama for All Ages**

"THE ARTWORK IS BEAUTIFUL; THE SHARP NOSES AND GLITTERY EYES ARE REMINISCENT OF RIYOKO IKEDA (THE ROSE OF VERSAILLES)."

– *Library Journal*

THANK GOD. IF YOU WEREN'T HOME, I WOULD HAVE HAD TO SHARE MY ROOM WITH THESE TWO.
RESTAURANT
DRIVE SAFE!
SURE YOU DON'T NEED A RIDE?
IT'S ONLY 10 MINUTES BY FOOT. I'LL WALK. IT'LL HELP ME SOBER UP A BIT.
I HAVE A SCORE TO SETTLE WITH THIS GUY ANYWAY.
WHY DIDN'T YOU INVITE ME ALONG TOO?
AREN'T YOU IN TRAINING? I HEARD COLLEGE LEAGUE HOCKEY WAS JUST AROUND THE CORNER.
AND STOP TRYING TO BUTT INTO ADULT GATHERINGS, LITTLE KID.
OKAY-, I'M GOING.
OKAY.
WAKE UP, SULYOUNG!
VROOM-

...ARE WE HOME...?
NO... WE'RE AT THE RIVERSIDE... I THOUGHT YOU SHOULD LET THE ALCOHOL WEAR OFF A BIT BEFORE WE HEAD HOME.
PHEW

...WAS I ASLEEP A LONG TIME?
IT'S YOUR SPECIALTY ALWAYS FALLING ASLEEP WHEN YOU'RE DRUNK.
...I'M THIRSTY.
WHY DID YOU DRINK SO MUCH?
IT WASN'T A LOT. I JUST... GOT DRUNK FOR SOME REASON.
...GOT A CIGARETTE?
FLIP
... YOUR BROTHER....

REALLY... LOVED RIVERS....
THAT'S WHY... I BURIED HIM BY THE RIVER...
BUT I REGRET THAT...
IF I KNEW HOW MUCH IT WOULD HURT WHENEVER I SEE A RIVER....
PUT ON YOUR SEATBELT! WE'RE LEAVING.
BRRAAOOOM

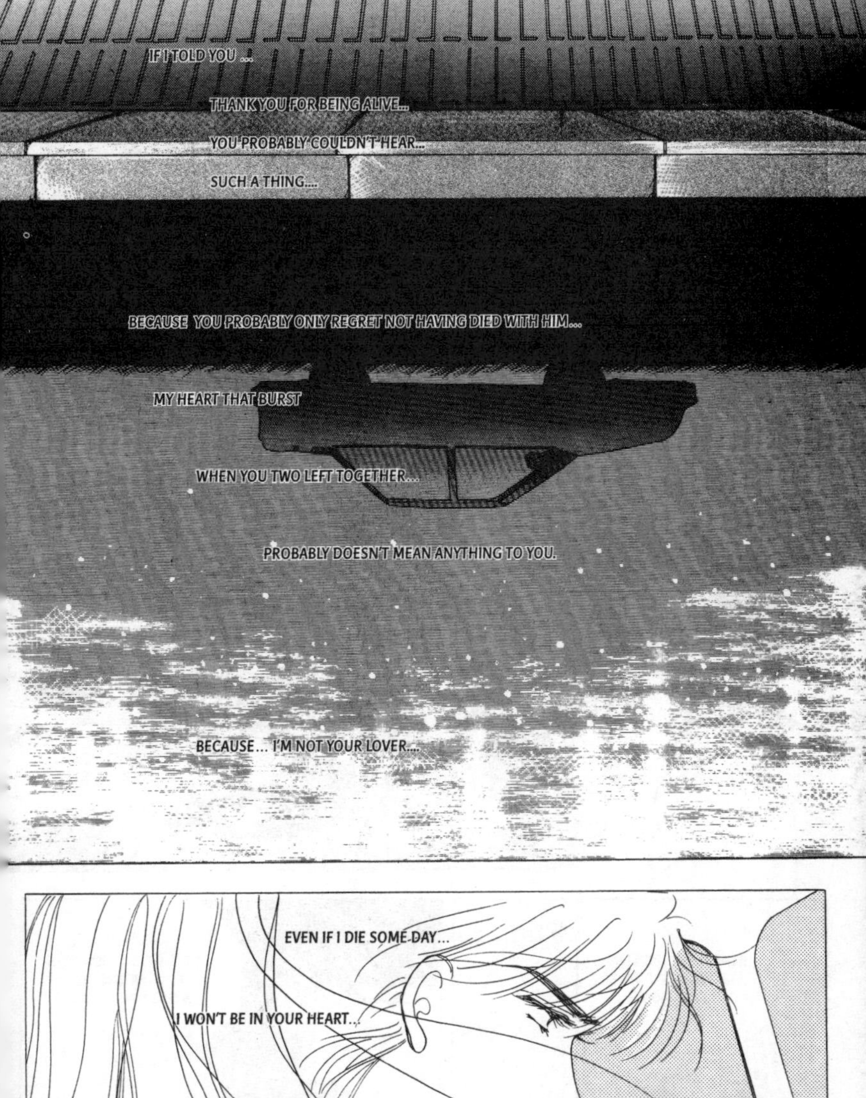
IF I TOLD YOU ...
THANK YOU FOR BEING ALIVE...
YOU PROBABLY COULDN'T HEAR...
SUCH A THING....
BECAUSE YOU PROBABLY ONLY REGRET NOT HAVING DIED WITH HIM...
MY HEART THAT BURST
WHEN YOU TWO LEFT TOGETHER...
PROBABLY DOESN'T MEAN ANYTHING TO YOU.
BECAUSE... I'M NOT YOUR LOVER...
EVEN IF I DIE SOME DAY...
I WON'T BE IN YOUR HEART...
BECAUSE... I'M NOT YOUR LOVER...

...WE COULD'VE HAD DINNER AT HOME.
FOR A STUDENT TO SPEND HIS MONEY AT A PLACE LIKE THIS....
WHEN IT'S JUST US, IT DOESN'T MATTER WHAT WE EAT. WE DIDN'T HAVE TO COME TO SUCH A FANCY-.
AREN'T YOU GOING TO EAT?
SINCE YOU ORDERED, I'LL EAT-. BUT DON'T DO THIS AGAIN-.
DO I STILL LOOK LIKE AN IMMATURE HIGH SCHOOLER TO YOU?

WHY CAN'T I BUY YOU DINNER FOR ONCE?
GANGBIN-, YOU KNOW THAT'S NOT WHAT I MEAN.
I WAS SAYING-.
-NO, I'M SORRY.
ALL RIGHT. THANK YOU.
NO MATTER WHAT I DO-
I ONLY LOOK LIKE A YOUNGER BROTHER TO YOU, HUH?
NO MATTER HOW MUCH I CHANGE, NO MATTER HOW OLD I GET.
I'M JUST... A YOUNGER BROTHER... IS THAT IT?
I'M SORRY IF I HURT YOUR FEELINGS.
DAMN IT!

YOUR MOTHER'S NOT BACK.
IS IT EXHIBITION SEASON?
WHAT ARE YOU DOING? COFFEE?
I WANT A DRINK.
WITHOUT ANY SNACKS? WE SHOULD HAVE HAD DRINKS WITH OUR DINNER THEN.
IT'S OKAY.
YOU GO UPSTAIRS AND DO YOUR THING.

ARE YOU... STILL ANGRY ABOUT THAT...?
...DON'T GET ANGRY... I'M SORRY.

I GUESS... I ONLY THINK ABOUT MYSELF.
BUT-.
GANGBIN....
I'M... STILL NOT MYSELF YET....
I'M NOT ANGRY AT YOU....
IF I COULD ONLY GET ANGRY AT HER...
IF I COULD GRAB HER AND SHAKE HER AND YELL AT HER TO PLEASE FORGET ABOUT HIM ALREADY...
THEN LOOK AT ME.

THE LOOK...
THAT COLDLY
SLASHES MY HEART...
WHEN I MEET THOSE EYES...
IT SHATTERS MY HEART
INTO A THOUSAND PIECES....
WHY...
DO YOU...
LOOK AT ME
LIKE THAT?

GANGBIN...
JUST-
BE STILL....
...GANGBIN....
PLEASE-
JUST BE STILL!

YOU'RE...
...LIKE MY YOUNGER BROTHER.
YEAH...
......
HOW THAT HURT ME SO MUCH...
YOU HAVE-NO-IDEA...
HOW MUCH THAT TORMENTED ME...
YOU'D NEVER KNOW, NOT IN A MILLION YEARS...
YOU PROBABLY DON'T KNOW THAT I WANTED TO DIE...
...GANGBIN....
MORE THAN YOU...
OH! YOU GUYS ARE BACK ALREADY.

*Cover not final

by Youngran Lee

"THIS STORY LOOKS LIKE IT IS GOING TO BE REALLY FUN. NICE ART, CUTE CHARACTERS, AND GENDER-BENDING, WHICH I ALWAYS LOVE.."

*– Rhonda Von Der Ahe, NETCOMICS subscriber*

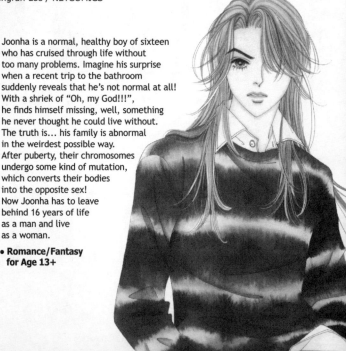

Joonha is a normal, healthy boy of sixteen who has cruised through life without too many problems. Imagine his surprise when a recent trip to the bathroom suddenly reveals that he's not normal at all! With a shriek of "Oh, my God!!!", he finds himself missing, well, something he never thought he could live without. The truth is... his family is abnormal in the weirdest possible way. After puberty, their chromosomes undergo some kind of mutation, which converts their bodies into the opposite sex! Now Joonha has to leave behind 16 years of life as a man and live as a woman.

- **Romance/Fantasy for Age 13+**

WHAT'S... GOING ON?
WHAT DO YOU THINK? AREN'T I PRETTY?
DO YOU THINK YOUR DAD WILL LIKE IT?
TA-DAH
CAN YOU PLEASE ACT YOUR AGE?
YOU'RE AN OLD WOMAN. THAT'S DISGUSTING.

I'M HUNGRY.
FEED ME.
YOU...
YOU...
YOU...
JERK...
SNIFF
SNIFF
TAP
TAP
PANT
PANT
HMPH
JOONHA'S DISSING
ME AGAIN!
COME OVER HERE!
SOB
SOB
HONEY!
BWAAA

JOONHA!
HE GOT SLOW. HE'S GETTING OLD.
RAT TAT TAT TAT
HE SAID THAT I'M OLD! AND DISGUSTING!
WHAT? HOW DARE YOU SAY SUCH OUTRAGEOUS THINGS TO HER!
DO YOU KNOW HOW HARD IT WAS FOR HER TO GIVE BIRTH TO YOU?
IT MAKES MY HEART ACHE WHENEVER I THINK ABOUT WHAT SHE WENT THROUGH!
MACK
SMACK
OTHER PEOPLE GIVE BIRTH, TOO! YOU'VE BEEN TALKING ABOUT THAT FOR THE LAST 16 YEARS! I'M SICK OF IT!
WHAT? YOU'RE SUCH A HORRIBLE, UNGRATEFUL SON!
SMACK
I STILL THINK YOUR MOTHER IS AN ANGEL! SHE'S BEAUTIFUL!
SMACK
SMACK
WHATEVER HAPPENED TO ALL THE ANGELS AND BEAUTIES?
SMACK
WHAT? WHY, YOU LITTLE...
JOONHA'S EVERYDAY LIFE

HMPH
THERE, THERE.
IT'S NOT HIS FIRST TIME DOING THIS. THERE, THERE.
PAT PAT
HE'S NOT AS STRONG AS HE USED TO BE. HE'S GETTING OLD.
← AFTER TEN YEARS OF GETTING BEATEN UP, HE CAN TAKE MOST OF THEM.
SURE, SURE. LET'S GO~♥
I DON'T WANT TO MAKE DINNER. LET'S GO WATCH A MOVIE.
TIRING...
IT'S FRIGGIN' TIRING TO LIVE WITH PARENTS WHO THINK LIKE ELEMENTARY SCHOOL KIDS.
SLAM

UH...
UH...
I'VE BEEN HAVING DIZZY SPELLS ONCE IN A WHILE.
BUT THEY'RE GETTING MORE AND MORE...
WHAT IF...
THERE'S SOMETHING WRONG WITH ME?

I FEEL TERRIBLE...

I FEEL LIKE MY BODY'S FLOATING IN AIR...

UM... HEY...

UH...UH...UH... UH, UH...

PLEASE... TAKE THIS!

WE'RE YOUR FANS...

THE POOh

THE POOH
DON'T YOU HAVE A MIRROR IN YOUR HOUSE?
HUH?
I SAID, DON'T YOU HAVE A MIRROR?
HOW DARE YOU APPROACH ME WITH YOUR UGLY FACES?! DOES YOUR BRAVERY COME FROM YOUR IGNORANCE?
GIVE YOURSELVES AN OBJECTIVE SELF EVALUATION AFTER LOOKING IN THE MIRROR IN YOUR CLASSROOM!

FROM NOW ON, DON'T EVEN LOOK AT MY FACE!

DON'T THINK ABOUT MY FACE OR MY NAME!

YOU'RE GETTING ON MY NERVES, OKAY?

AS IF I DON'T FEEL CRAPPY ALREADY. I DON'T NEED YOU TO PISS ME OFF!

JERK...

IS THAT ALL YOU CAN SAY TO THE GIRLS WHO LIKE YOU?

HMPH!

BEING AN UGLY GIRL IS A CRIME.

BY THE WAY...
YOU DON'T LOOK TOO WELL.
I'VE BEEN LIKE THIS SINCE MORNING... DAMN IT!
I WAS ON MY WAY TO THE NURSE'S OFFICE.

I FEEL AWFUL...
MAYBE I'M COMING DOWN WITH A COLD.
IT FEELS LIKE...
JOONHA...
MY BODY'S FLOATING...
UH... HUH?

JOONHA!

AH...
MNG
MNG
OH... UH...
THIS REALLY HURTS..
HUFF
HUFF
GOSH...

DAMN IT! MY BODY FEELS LIKE IT'S BEING TORN APART...
NNG
NNG
INTO TWO PIECES...
AM I GOING TO...
DIE LIKE THIS?
IF I KNEW I WAS GOING TO DIE LIKE THIS...
I LIKE YOU...
HEEWON...

I SHOULD'VE...

KISSED HER AT LEAST...

JINHOO...
I THINK I'M DYING...
UH...I'M STILL WORRIED ABOUT JOONHA.. HIS FEVER WENT UP TO 40 DEGREES.
THE DOCTOR SAID HE SHOULD BE HOSPITALIZED, BUT YOU BROUGHT HIM HOME...
THAT'S OKAY, THAT'S OKAY.
MOM
HE'LL GET WELL, AND YOU'LL SEE HIM AT SCHOOL IN A FEW DAYS.
NO PAIN, NO GAIN.
THAT'S RIGHT!
CAN JOONNA REALLY LIVE?

HOW SAD...HE THINKS OF HIS FRIEND MORE THAN HIS PARENTS IN TIMES OF PAIN...

MOM...
MOM...
I... SOMEWHAT FEEL EMPTY...
FEELS LIKE I JUST HAD A NIGHT-MARE...
. . . .

THEY MUST'VE LEFT THEIR SICK SON BEHIND TO GO ON A DATE.
OH WELL...
THIS ISN'T THE FIRST TIME THEY'VE BEEN UNCONCERNED ABOUT THEIR SON.
SCRATCH SCRATCH
SLAM
THIS IS THE RESTROOM
THIS IS THE RESTROOM
AAAAAAAA

AHHHH
AAAACK
AAACK
HUH?
AAAACK~
JOONHA?
AAAACK!
WHAT... WHAT... WHAT I NEED TO PEE... WITH...
THIS IS CRAZY! I...I'M GONE!
OH, THAT?
I...I...I...I...
...I... I'M GONE!
I...I...I...I... WAS TRYING TO PEE...AND...
THIS...THIS IS A NIGHTMARE... IT'S A LIE...
THIS CAN'T BE... IT'S A NIGHTMARE ... A NIGHTMARE ... A NIGHT ...
THIS CAN'T BE...
IT'S A NIGHTMARE... A NIGHTMARE... A NIGHT...
SWOOSH

THUMP
JOONHA!
YOU'RE OVERREACTING...
ARE YOU AWAKE NOW?

AAAACK
ZAP
THIS IS THE RESTROOM
SLAM
IT... WASN'T A DREAM!
THIS CAN'T BE HAPPENING... WHAT SHOULD I DO... WHAT SHOULD I DO...
HOW CAN THIS HAPPEN?
MY... MY PLUMBING, MY LITTLE GUY HAS BEEN STOLEN... THIS CAN'T BE...

I'M CRIPPLED NOW! I'M NOT A MAN ANYMORE! I'M DEFORMED!

I'M IMPOTENT! I'M AN EUNUCH!

THIS CAN'T BE HAPPENING! THIS IS A NIGHTMARE! MY THING'S GONE!

IT WAS TOO SMALL TO MAKE A DIFFERENCE IN THE FIRST PLACE ANYWAY... STOP OVERREACTING...

IT'S NOTHING SERIOUS.

THE CHROMOSOME CHANGE RUNS IN OUR FAMILY.

WHAT?

# Roureville

by E.Hae

"I MUST CONFESS THAT THIS IS ONE STORY THAT CAN GROW ON A READER."

– Antoinette Lyles, NETCOMICS subscriber

From the bestselling creator of *Not So Bad* comes *Roureville*, a mysterious fantasy drama with a shonen-ai undertone. Evan Price is a celebrated New York Times reporter who has been ordered by his editor to cover an out-of-state story: "real" ghost sightings in a secluded village in the countryside. After ten days of driving by sleepy rural villages with zero results, our lost and exhausted New Yorker is just about ready to give up. But then suddenly, a road sign pointing to "Roureville" catches his eye. Little does he know that the end of his long road trip is just the beginning of an incredible tale.

- **Shonen-ai/Fantasy for Age 16+**

ROUREVILLE #02
EVAN PRYCE.

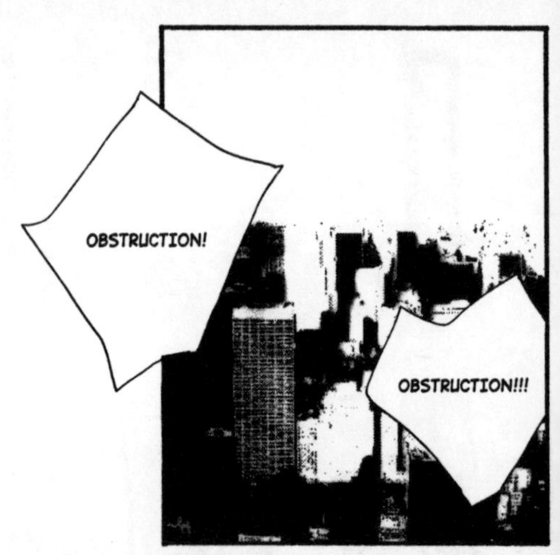

OBSTRUCTION!
OBSTRUCTION!!!

NEW YORK

THIS IS CLEARLY AN OBSTRUCTION OF WORK, PRYCE.

GRIN
BUT I WORK HERE.

HERE...

HEY, GET ME SOMETHING TO DRINK.

DON'T YOU HAVE GINSENG TEA INSTEAD OF COFFEE?

AND AS FOR BOTTLED WATER, I WOULD LIKE AN EVIAN.

OH YEAH, AND DON'T FORGET TO GET ME SOME ROYAL MILK TEA LATER.

ZAP

ZAP

GRRR

BOSS

YOU!! WHY AREN'T YOU OUTSIDE COVERING A STORY? GET THE HELL OUT!

BARK

EEP

SNIFF

AND WHY IS IT SO HOT IN HERE?

KROOSH

KROOSH

PRYCE SAID HE HAS ASTHMA AND THE BREEZE FROM THE AC WON'T BE GOOD FOR HIS HEALTH....

THE HEAT JUST COMES BLAZING IN.

AND YOU BELIEVED THAT?

SLURP

IF YOU BROKE A DANGEROUS STORY YOU SHOULD BE IN HIDING!

WHY ARE YOU DOING THIS IN THE OFFICE?

THIS ISN'T YOUR PERSONAL HOTEL, PRYCE!

GROWL!!

NOBODY CAN DO ANY WORK AROUND HERE BECAUSE OF YOU!

WELL...

...I'M JUST REALLY BORED.

(NOT!)

POOF!

I'VE BEEN WORKING SO HARD ON THAT STORY FOR SO LONG, I'VE GOT NOTHING TO DO DURING MY TIME OFF.

(NOT!)

NO SMOKI

THIS PLACE IS SMOKE FREE!

COME ON~. IT'S NOT GOOD FOR YOUR HEALTH TO GET ANGRY AT EVERY LITTLE THING, BOSS.

TAP TAP

BECAUSE OF THIS GROUND-BREAKING ARTICLE, I HEARD THAT TERRORISTS AND DRUG DEALERS

ARE JUST ITCHING TO GET THEIR HANDS ON YOU, SO WHY ARE YOU PRETENDING TO BE HIDING HERE?

THIS IS EXACTLY THE KIND OF PLACE THEY LEAST EXPECT TO FIND ME.

KE KE

HOTELS ARE TOO STIFLING. AND I DON'T LIKE PLANE RIDES EITHER.

LOOK HERE! THIS ISN'T A JOKE.

THEY HAVE A BOUNTY ON YOUR HEAD.

ACK ACK
SLUMP
THUMP
COUGH
PUHAHAHAHA
DO YOU REALLY THINK THE "INFAMOUS" "RIGHT-WINGED SOUTH AMERICAN ASSASSINS" WILL "BLOW UP THIS WHOLE BUILDING" JUST TO KILL ME?
AWW~ COME ON, BOSS~
R~R R
LENCE~
SMIRK
SI-
HELLO.
YES, THIS IS THE NEW YORK TIMES. GO AHEAD.
R R
R R
R
HEY, DON'T YOU GUYS HAVE WORK TO DO? WHAT ARE YOU LOOKING AT?
CLICK
R R
R R
R R
...

WHAT? GHOSTS?
AND YOU CALLED THE NEW YORK TIMES FOR THAT? WHY YOU....
WAIT.
?
WHERE IS IT?
BUT MY LIFE IS IN DANGER...
AS OF YESTERDAY DOTON HAS TURNED INTO AN IMBECILE AND HE'S BEEN TYPING THE SAME SENTENCES OVER AND OVER AGAIN.
AND RICHARD WAS TAKEN TO THE HOSPITAL DUE TO STOMACH CRAMPS.
NOBODY CAN TAKE CARE OF THEMSELVES AROUND HERE.
PRYCE, YOU NEED TO GO CHECK IT OUT.
HEARD IT'S A SMALL VILLAGE, NOT EVEN ON THE MAP. THE TERRORISTS WILL NEVER FIND YOU THERE!
THE ONLY GUYS WE CAN SEND TO TRACK DOWN STORIES ARE SAYING THEY'RE NOT COMING BACK AS LONG AS YOU'RE STILL HERE...
AND A LOT OF PEOPLE ARE SHOWING SIGNS OF NERVOUSNESS AND PARANOIA.
SO THAT LEAVES YOU!
YOU SAID HOTELS ARE STIFLING THIS IS YOUR LUCKY DAY!
HA HA HA

THAT'S VERY GOOD, PRYCE-.
SURE THING. EVEN THE NEW YORK TIMES NEED A HORROR FLICK OR TWO.
GHOSTS! WHAT A GREAT SUBJECT!
I GUESS IT'LL BE BETTER THAN USING THIS PLACE AS A HOTEL FOR MONTHS TO COME!
IT'S BEEN A WEEK SINCE I STARTED EATING AND SLEEPING IN THE OFFICE.
YOU'RE SENDING ME, EVAN PRYCE, TO COVER A FLIMSY STORY LIKE THAT?
HU
I SUPPOSE I'LL GO.
PBT PBT
NO HOPE...
PANT PANT
THUMP THUMP
GULP
THEN...
TAP
TAP
TAP
...CAN BE FOUND HERE EITHER.
CAN I TURN THE AC BACK ON?
THERE'S A REWARD OUT FOR HIS DEATH.
THAT MAN WILL SELL HIS GRANDMOTHER IF HE NEEDS TO. SO JUST WORRY ABOUT YOURSELF, OKAY?
DO YOU THINK HE'LL BE OKAY?

HAH
TZZZ
SERIOUSLY...
HE IS GIFTED IN THESE SORTS OF THINGS...
THE OFFICE IS SMOKE-FREE.
...
NOTHING IS IMPOSSIBLE ONCE YOU PUT YOUR MIND TO IT.
BUT, THEN AGAIN...
SOMEWHERE BETWEEN THE STATE OF CALIFORNIA AND YELLOW STONE NATIONAL PARK....
HOW CAN DRIVING DIRECTIONS BE SO VAGUE?

IT'S BEEN TEN DAYS SINCE I SET OFF TO TRACK THIS STORY.

AND I HAVE YET TO FIND MY DESTINATION: ROUREVILLE.

MAYBE I SHOULD HAVE EXPECTED THIS SINCE THE PLACE ISN'T ON THE MAP.

I HAVE NO CLUE AS TO WHERE IT IS, OR WHAT ROUREVILLE STANDS FOR.

MAYBE I UNDERESTIMATED THIS PROJECT....

BA
IT WAS A HALF-ASSED PROJECT TO KILL SOME TIME, BUT THE PAST TEN DAYS WERE FAR FROM EASY.
I MAY HAVE HEARD OF IT... I'M NOT SURE. WHY DON'T YOU WATCH OUR MAGIC SHOW AND REST A BIT?

I'M ACTUALLY ON MY WAY TO PARIS... PARIS, TEXAS I MEAN... HMM...
DON'T KNOW NOTHIN' 'BOUT NO ROUREVILLE, BUT YOU WON' HAPPEN TO BE GOING TO IDAHO, ARE YA?

AFTER GOING THROUGH A NUMBER OF SMALL TOWNS,

I WAS ABLE TO SPEAK TO SOMEONE WHO HAD HEARD OF A PLACE SIMILAR TO WHAT I WAS LOOKING FOR. THAT WAS THREE DAYS AGO.

COVERING THIS STORY WAS ONLY AN EXCUSE, SO NOBODY'LL COMPLAIN IF I WENT BACK EMPTY-HANDED.
I'VE BEEN AWAY FOR TEN DAYS, WHICH MEANS I DID ALL I COULD.
SHOULD I JUST GIVE UP?
BUT SO FAR, I HAVEN'T SEEN ANYTHING CLOSE.
WHERE AM I SUPPOSED TO STAY TONIGHT?
CAN'T FIND A DECENT MOTEL AND I'M OUT OF GAS.
CLUNK
CLUNK
CLUNK
CLUNK
WHEEEE...
CLUNK
WHEEEE...
WHEEEE...
CLUNK
CLUNK
...

IS THERE A VILLAGE CALLED ROUREVILLE AROUND HERE?
SWISH
WHEEE
WHAT IS IT?
HELLO, FATHER!
CLUNK
CAN I ASK YOU FOR DIRECTIONS?
GLANCE
WHY DO YOU WANT TO GO THERE?
ROUREVILLE...
WHEEEEE...
SSSSS
YOU BETTER GET AWAY FROM HERE BEFORE SOMETHING BAD HAPPENS TO YOU....
WHEEEEE...
WA... WAIT...
GHOSTS? THAT'S SACRILEGIOUS!
I'VE NEVER SEEN OR HEARD OF A PLACE LIKE THAT.
I'M EVAN PRYCE FROM THE NEW YORK TIMES. WE HAVE INFORMATION THAT GHOSTS APPEAR IN....
HAH!

I BETTER FIND SOMEWHERE TO STAY BEFORE IT GETS DARK.

WHEEEE~

...

OW!

A SANDSTORM?

THAT GUY BOTHERS THE HELL OUT OF ME...

MAYBE I SHOULD GO DOWN THAT BYPATH THE OLD PRIEST DISAPPEARED INTO.

ROUREVILLE...
...
ROUREVIL
SWISH
...
A BROKEN SIGN THAT HASN'T BEEN REPLACED...

A SECLUDED VILLAGE—JUST AS I EXPECTED.
IRENE'S
HELLO~♪
WHY THAT STUPID, LYING PRIEST!!
BAD THINGS WILL HAPPEN TO ME. MY ASS!!

RING THIS UP, PLEASE.
GLANCE
SWISH
I GUESS PEOPLE DO LIVE HERE.
THIS IS YOUR FIRST TIME IN ROUREVILLE. ISN'T IT?
SHE'S CUTE. A RARE FIND IN A COUNTRY TOWN LIKE THIS.
BABY FACE AND WITH A CIGARETTE.
AN INTERESTING COMBINATION. I LIKE IT.
YEAH, I THINK I TOOK A WRONG TURN.
IS THERE ANYWHERE I CAN STAY?

OH NO-

I'M SORRY, BUT THIS IS SUCH A SMALL VILLAGE THAT WE DON'T HAVE ANY LODGING FACILITIES.

IT'LL BE BETTER FOR YOU TO GET ON THE HIGHWAY AND FIND A MOTEL BEFORE THE SUN GOES DOWN.

REALLY... I'VE RUN OUT OF GAS, TOO... DAMMIT.

NOW THAT I THINK ABOUT IT, I HEARD SOMETHING INTERESTING ABOUT THIS PLACE.

ABOUT GHOSTS SHOWING UP...

THUD

MERC

67

IT EVEN HAS A NAME, ACCORDING TO THE STORY...

JESS...? JAMES... WAS IT?

HMM

I DON'T KNOW WHERE YOU GOT THAT INFORMATION, BUT-

OH.

HUHU

SPEAK OF THE DEVIL-

WHY DON'T YOU CHECK IT OUT?

SLIDE
FOR YOURSELF?

THIS WAS MY FIRST
ENCOUNTER WITH HIM.
See what happens next at www.NETCOMICS.com!

## Shonen-ai

### *Boy Princess*
by Seyoung Kim

*Boy Princess* is a pulse-quickening tale of swords and sorcery, far-away kingdoms, and the fairest princess in all the land. Except...this is a fairy tale with a twist. When a prince's soon-to-be-bride elopes two days before their wedding, her desperate family dresses up their young son and send him to get married in her place. But how long can he keep up the charade?

• **Shonen-ai/Fantasy for Age 13+**

### *Let Dai*
by Sooyeon Won

*Let Dai* is a tragic tale of forbidden love and unforgivable betrayal. Set in a soulless neo-Seoul ruled by young punks and pleasure seekers, an amoral teenager named Dai is the living embodiment of the city's beauty and cruelty, as the leader of the vicious Furies gang. When a schoolboy, Jaehee rescues a beautiful girl from the Furies, he can't possibly realize how this brief encounter will plunge him into a downward spiral into the unknown.

• **Shonen-ai/Drama for Age 16+**

### *Not So Bad*
by E.HAE

Eunhee is a rich superstar. Gain is a homeless vagabond. By a whimsical twist of events and a moment of caprice, they find themselves sharing Eunhee's cozy bachelor's pad. Eunhee's apartment is enough for two, but there is only one bedroom, the nights have grown cold, and snuggling next to the oblivious Eunhee's warm body seems to be the only cure to Gain's recurring insomnia...

• **Shonen-ai/Drama for Age 16+**

**Available now at your favorite bookstores.**
**Read it online at www.NETCOMICS.com!**

## *AEGIS*

by Jinha Yoo

A grand-scale masterpiece of life in a dystopian future, *AEGIS* paints a picture of the love and friendship between orphans Jino and Izare. The earth secretly trains an army of boys. Jino and Izare are abandoned at the camp, but only Jino escapes the soul-killing cruelty of the camp. With Jino in his heart, Izare remains to become an ultimate weapon. The boy's lives, and the secrets of the mysterious Maria, gradually unravel. For Earth, can peace be won?

- **SF/Fantasy for Age 16+**

"THE STORY RELIES A LOT MORE ON ACTION AND THIS ONGOING FEELING OF 'SOMETHING GREATER' THAT IS GOING TO UNFOLD SOON, CREATING A NICE, SUSPENSEFUL MOOD..."

*– AnimeOnDVD.com*

## *LETHE*

by Kimjin

Mazda Hun is a soldier caught in a web of political and military struggles beyond his comprehension. Captured by the government, they sentence him to Lethe. Society doesn't believe in the death penalty anymore. They've modernized the paradigm of punishment. Lethe has many names: mercy, treatment, repair, reformation and rehabilitation. Some even call it justice. Lethe is the execution of a person's soul. Those who undergo the process don't seem quite human ever again.

- **SF for Age 16+**

"THE ART FOR THIS TITLE IS BEAUTIFULLY COLORED AND INTERESTING IN ITS REPETITION AND GESTURED, MORPHING LINES."

*– Amanda Sowers, NETCOMICS subscriber*

**Available now at your favorite bookstores.**
**Read it online at www.NETCOMICS.com!**

# Emperor's Castle

Chunhoo Kang thrives in a world of crime, sex and intrigue. He's the Nihon Saikono Warrior, Japan's greatest fighter in the yakuza underworld. However, he's also Korean. Haunted by past sins, Chunhoo abandons his life of crime to search for the young woman and son he forsook decades ago. Unfortunately, his yakuza bosses are unforgiving, and assassins trail him all the way back to Korea. But Chunhoo is determined not to be anybody's servant anymore. He's going to become an Emperor and found his own empire.

- **Action for Age 16+**

"A GOOD, GRITTY, YAKUZA STYLE STORY WITH STRONG ART."

– *Jarred Pine, NETCOMICS subscriber*

**Available now at your favorite bookstores.**
**Read it online at www.NETCOMICS.com!**

# NETCOMICS 2007 Release Schedule

| Ship Date | ISBN-13 | Title | Author | US Retail |
|---|---|---|---|---|
| 01/07 | 978-1-60009-090-5 | In the Starlight Vol. 1 | Kyungok Kang | $9.99 |
| 01/07 | 978-1-60009-122-3 | Narration of Love at 17 Vol. 3 | Kyungok Kang | $9.99 |
| 01/07 | 978-1-60009-024-0 | 0/6 (Zero/Six) Vol. 5 | Youjung Lee | $9.99 |
| 01/07 | 978-1-60009-034-9 | Boy Princess Vol. 5 | Seyoung Kim | $9.99 |
| 01/07 | 978-1-60009-009-7 | Let Dai Vol. 5 | Sooyeon Won | $9.99 |
| 02/07 | 978-1-60009-216-9 | 100% Perfect Girl Vol. 1 | Wann | $9.99 |
| 02/07 | 978-1-60009-209-1 | Roureville Vol. 1 | E.Hae | $9.99 |
| 02/07 | 978-1-60009-125-4 | Let's be Perverts Vol. 2 | Youjung Lee | $9.99 |
| 02/07 | 978-1-60009-059-2 | Emperor's Castle Vol. 3 | Sungmo Kim | $9.99 |
| 02/07 | 978-1-60009-049-3 | Land of Silver Rain Vol. 5 | Mira Lee | $9.99 |
| 02/07 | 978-1-60009-069-1 | Pine Kiss Vol. 5 | Eunhye Lee | $9.99 |
| 03/07 | 978-1-60009-183-4 | 10, 20, and 30 Vol. 1 | Morim Kang | $9.99 |
| 03/07 | 978-1-60009-201-5 | Click Vol. 1 | Youngran Lee | $9.99 |
| 03/07 | 978-1-60009-141-4 | June Vol. 2 | Youngran Lee | $9.99 |
| 03/07 | 978-1-60009-043-1 | Can't Lose You Vol. 5 | Wann | $9.99 |
| 03/07 | 978-1-60009-079-0 | Dokebi Bride Vol. 5 | Marley | $9.99 |
| 03/07 | 978-1-60009-004-2 | The Great Catsby Vol. 5 | Doha | $19.99 |
| 03/07 | 978-1-60009-035-6 | Boy Princess Vol. 6 | Seyoung Kim | $9.99 |
| 03/07 | 978-1-60009-010-3 | Let Dai Vol. 6 | Sooyeon Won | $9.99 |
| 04/07 | 978-1-60009-091-2 | In the Starlight Vol. 2 | Kyungok Kang | $9.99 |
| 04/07 | 978-1-60009-192-6 | Your Lover Vol. 3 | Seungwon Han | $9.99 |
| 04/07 | 978-1-60009-103-2 | AEGIS Vol. 4 | Jinha Yoo | $9.99 |
| 04/07 | 978-1-60009-123-0 | Narration of Love at 17 Vol. 4 | Kyungok Kang | $9.99 |
| 05/07 | 978-1-60009-116-2 | Two Will Come Vol. 1 | Kyungok Kang | $9.99 |
| 05/07 | 978-1-60009-217-6 | 100% Perfect Girl Vol. 2 | Wann | $9.99 |
| 05/07 | 978-1-60009-126-1 | Let's be Perverts Vol. 3 | Youjung Lee | $9.99 |
| 05/07 | 978-1-60009-060-8 | Emperor's Castle Vol. 4 | Sungmo Kim | $9.99 |
| 05/07 | 978-1-60009-050-9 | Land of Silver Rain Vol. 6 | Mira Lee | $9.99 |
| 05/07 | 978-1-60009-070-7 | Pine Kiss Vol. 6 | Eunhye Lee | $9.99 |
| 05/07 | 978-1-60009-036-3 | Boy Princess Vol. 7 | Seyoung Kim | $9.99 |
| 05/07 | 978-1-60009-011-0 | Let Dai Vol. 7 | Sooyeon Won | $9.99 |
| 06/07 | 978-1-60009-184-1 | 10, 20, and 30 Vol. 2 | Morim Kang | $9.99 |
| 06/07 | 978-1-60009-202-2 | Click Vol. 2 | Youngran Lee | $9.99 |
| 06/07 | 978-1-60009-210-7 | Roureville Vol. 2 | E.Hae | $9.99 |
| 06/07 | 978-1-60009-044-8 | Can't Lose You Vol. 6 | Wann | $9.99 |
| 06/07 | 978-1-60009-080-6 | Dokebi Bride Vol. 6 | Marley | $9.99 |
| 06/07 | 978-1-60009-052-3 | The Great Catsby Vol. 6 | Doha | $24.99 |

| Ship Date | ISBN-13 | Title | Author | US Retail |
|---|---|---|---|---|
| 07/07 | 978-1-60009-251-0 | Kingdom of the Winds Vol. 1 | Kimjin | TBA |
| 07/07 | 978-1-60009-231-2 | Operation Liberate Men Vol. 1 | Mira Lee | $9.99 |
| 07/07 | 978-1-60009-092-9 | In the Starlight Vol. 3 | Kyungok Kang | $9.99 |
| 07/07 | 978-1-60009-129-2 | Almost Highly Classified Vol. 2 | JTK | $17.99 |
| 07/07 | 978-1-60009-142-1 | June Vol. 3 | Youngran Lee | $9.99 |
| 07/07 | 978-1-60009-037-0 | Boy Princess Vol. 8 | Seyoung Kim | $9.99 |
| 07/07 | 978-1-60009-012-7 | Let Dai Vol. 8 | Sooyeon Won | $9.99 |
| 08/07 | 978-1-60009-117-9 | Two Will Come Vol. 2 | Kyungok Kang | $9.99 |
| 08/07 | 978-1-60009-218-3 | 100% Perfect Girl Vol. 3 | Wann | $9.99 |
| 08/07 | 978-1-60009-127-8 | Let's be Perverts Vol. 4 | Youjung Lee | $9.99 |
| 08/07 | 978-1-60009-193-3 | Your Lover Vol. 4 | Seungwon Han | $9.99 |
| 08/07 | 978-1-60009-061-5 | Emperor's Castle Vol. 5 | Sungmo Kim | $9.99 |
| 08/07 | 978-1-60009-104-9 | AEGIS Vol. 5 | Jinha Yoo | $9.99 |
| 08/07 | 978-1-60009-051-6 | Land of Silver Rain Vol. 7 | Mira Lee | $9.99 |
| 08/07 | 978-1-60009-071-4 | Pine Kiss Vol. 7 | Eunhye Lee | $9.99 |
| 09/07 | 978-1-60009-185-8 | 10, 20, and 30 Vol. 3 | Morim Kang | $9.99 |
| 09/07 | 978-1-60009-203-9 | Click Vol. 3 | Youngran Lee | $9.99 |
| 09/07 | 978-1-60009-081-3 | Dokebi Bride Vol. 7 | Marley | $9.99 |
| 09/07 | 978-1-60009-038-7 | Boy Princess Vol. 9 | Seyoung Kim | $9.99 |
| 09/07 | 978-1-60009-013-4 | Let Dai Vol. 9 | Sooyeon Won | $9.99 |
| 10/07 | 978-1-60009-177-3 | Passionate Two-Face Vol. 1 | Youjung Lee | $9.99 |
| 10/07 | 978-1-60009-252-7 | Kingdom of the Winds Vol. 2 | Kimjin | TBA |
| 10/07 | 978-1-60009-232-9 | Operation Liberate Men Vol. 2 | Mira Lee | $9.99 |
| 10/07 | 978-1-60009-093-6 | In the Starlight Vol. 4 | Kyungok Kang | $9.99 |
| 11/07 | 978-1-60009-118-6 | Two Will Come Vol. 3 | Kyungok Kang | $9.99 |
| 11/07 | 978-1-60009-211-4 | Roureville Vol. 3 | E.Hae | $9.99 |
| 11/07 | 978-1-60009-219-0 | 100% Perfect Girl Vol. 4 | Wann | $9.99 |
| 11/07 | 978-1-60009-143-8 | June Vol. 4 | Youngran Lee | $9.99 |
| 11/07 | 978-1-60009-062-2 | Emperor's Castle Vol. 6 | Sungmo Kim | $9.99 |
| 11/07 | 978-1-60009-072-1 | Pine Kiss Vol. 8 | Eunhye Lee | $9.99 |
| 11/07 | 978-1-60009-014-1 | Let Dai Vol. 10 | Sooyeon Won | $9.99 |
| 12/07 | 978-1-60009-186-5 | 10, 20, and 30 Vol. 4 | Morim Kang | $9.99 |
| 12/07 | 978-1-60009-204-6 | Click Vol. 4 | Youngran Lee | $9.99 |
| 12/07 | 978-1-60009-105-6 | AEGIS Vol. 6 | Jinha Yoo | $9.99 |
| 12/07 | 978-1-60009-082-0 | Dokebi Bride Vol. 8 | Marley | $9.99 |